To all lovers of art

by Victoria Sara Dazin

This book is dedicated to my son Guy.

My Paintings and Drawings is a collection of several portraits I sketched, draw and painted, that I using various techniques and materials such as black, color pencils and pastel oil on Steinbach paper, aquarelle on Saunders Waterford and oil on canvas.

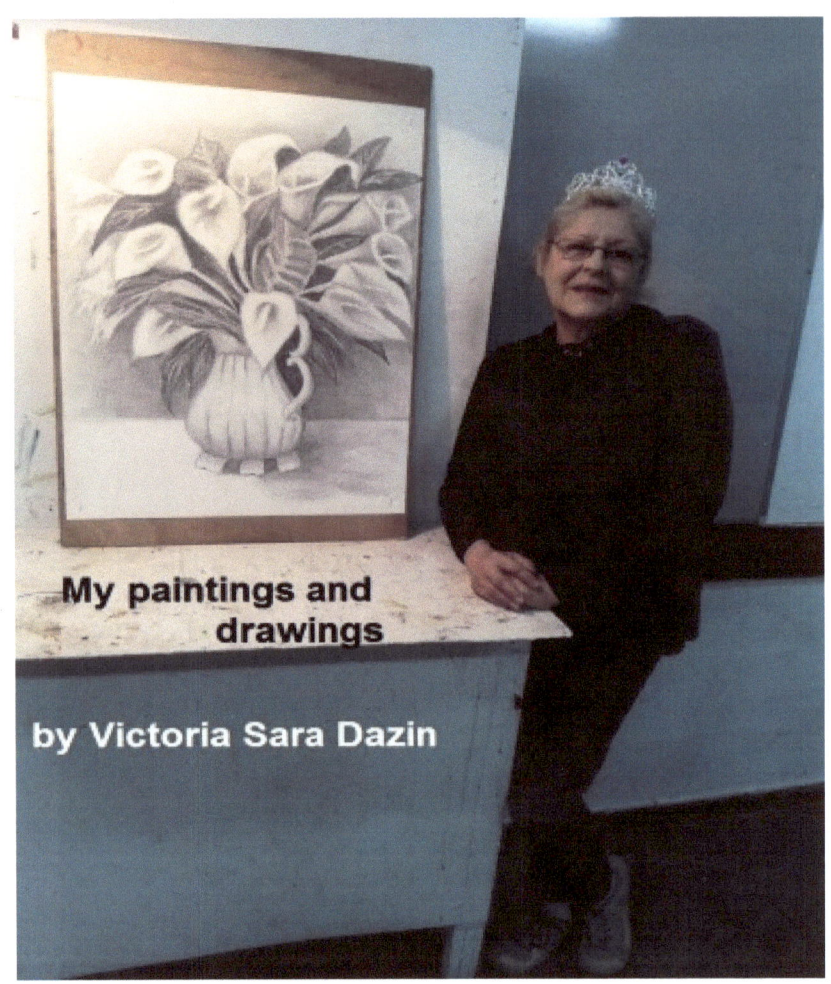

My paintings and drawings

by Victoria Sara Dazin

Part 1

My black pencil's drawings

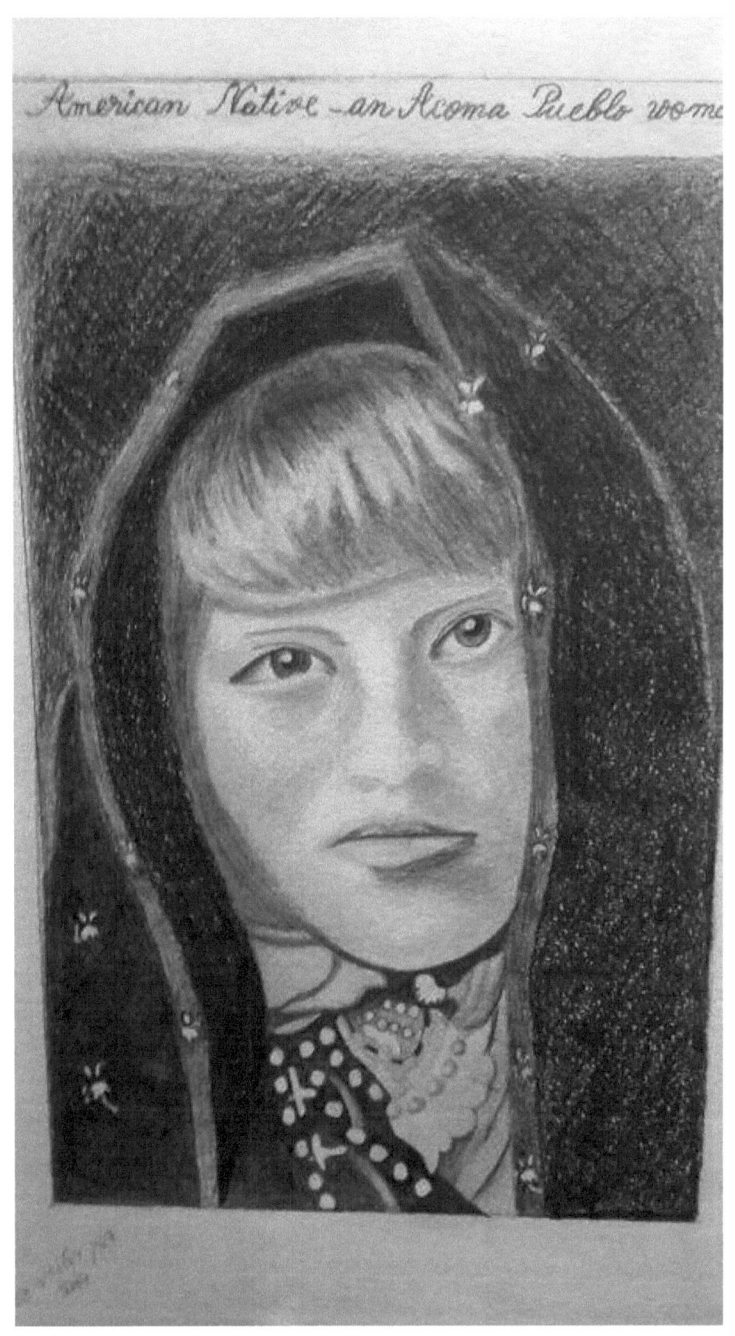

American Native woman - an Acoma Pueblo woman.

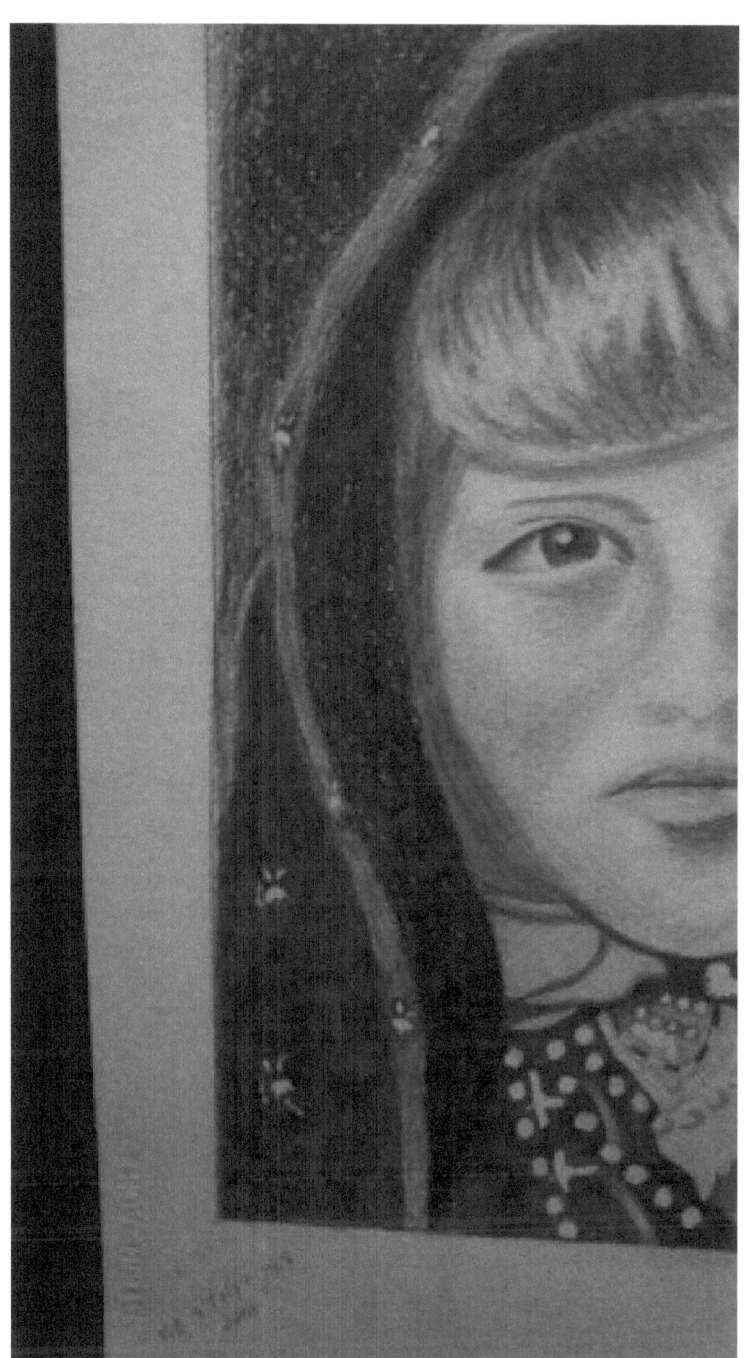

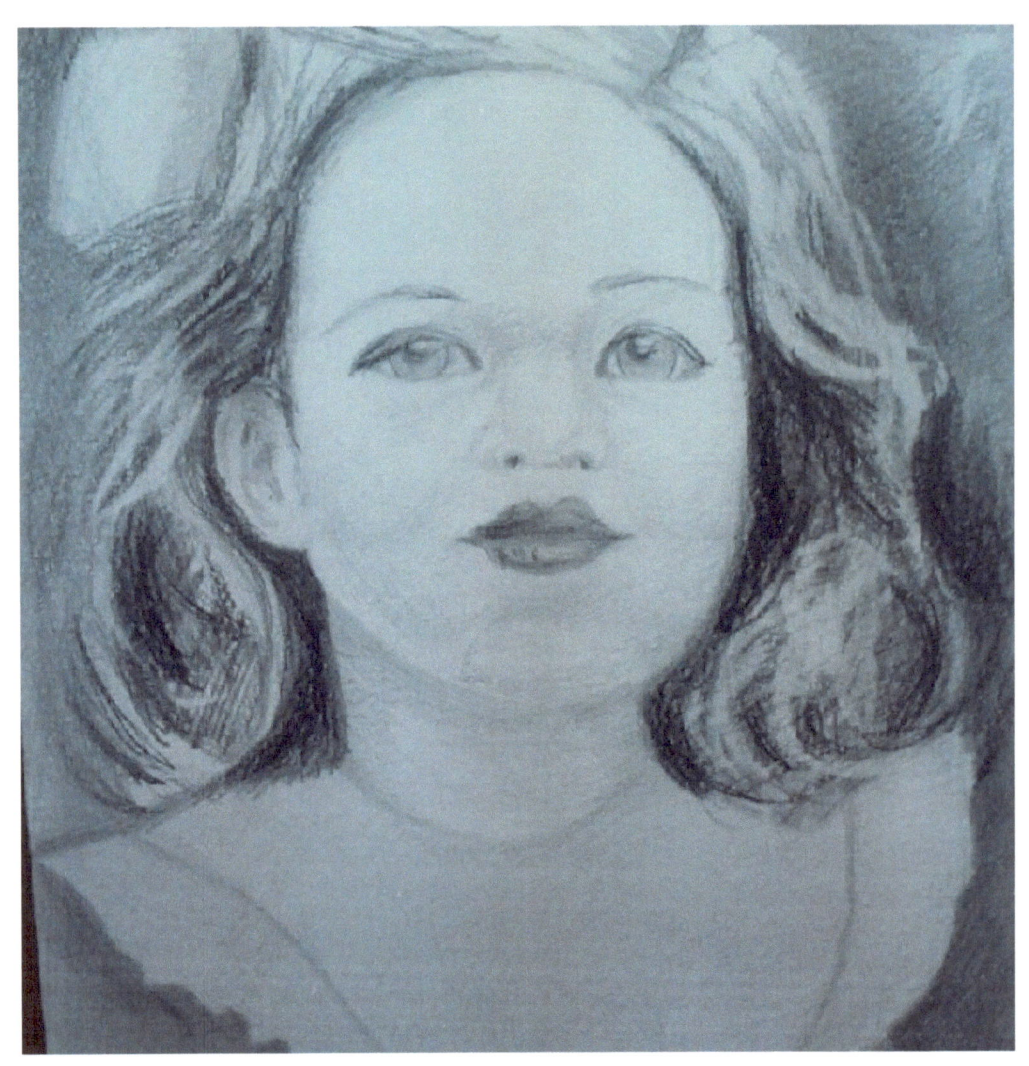

A little girl

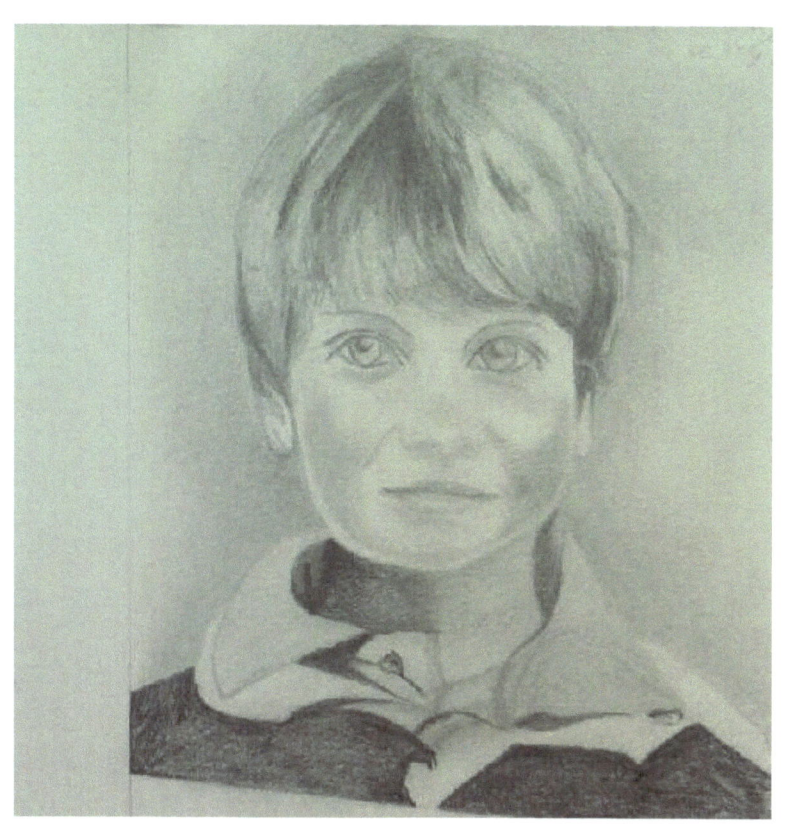

A boy

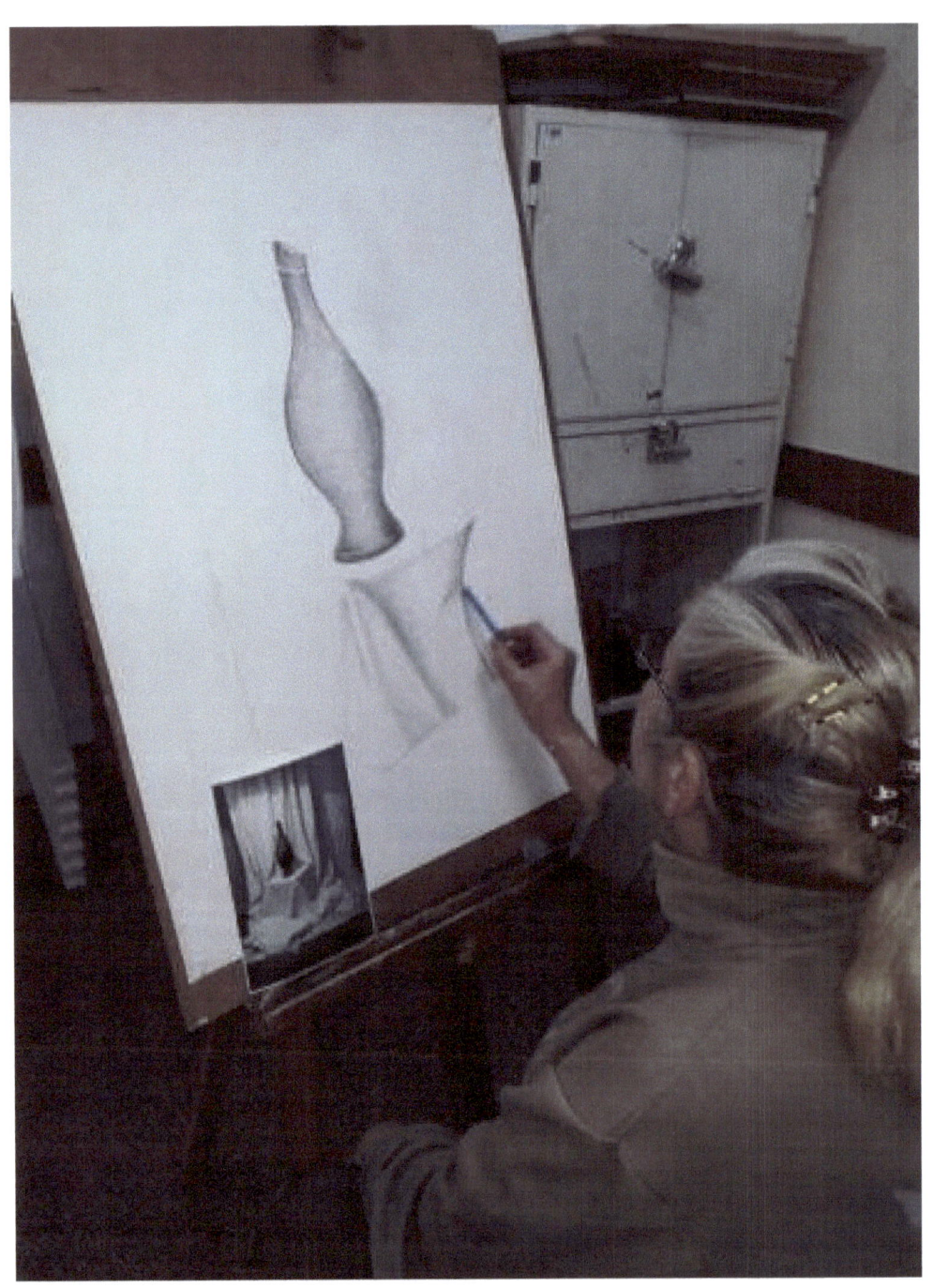

Drawing in progress

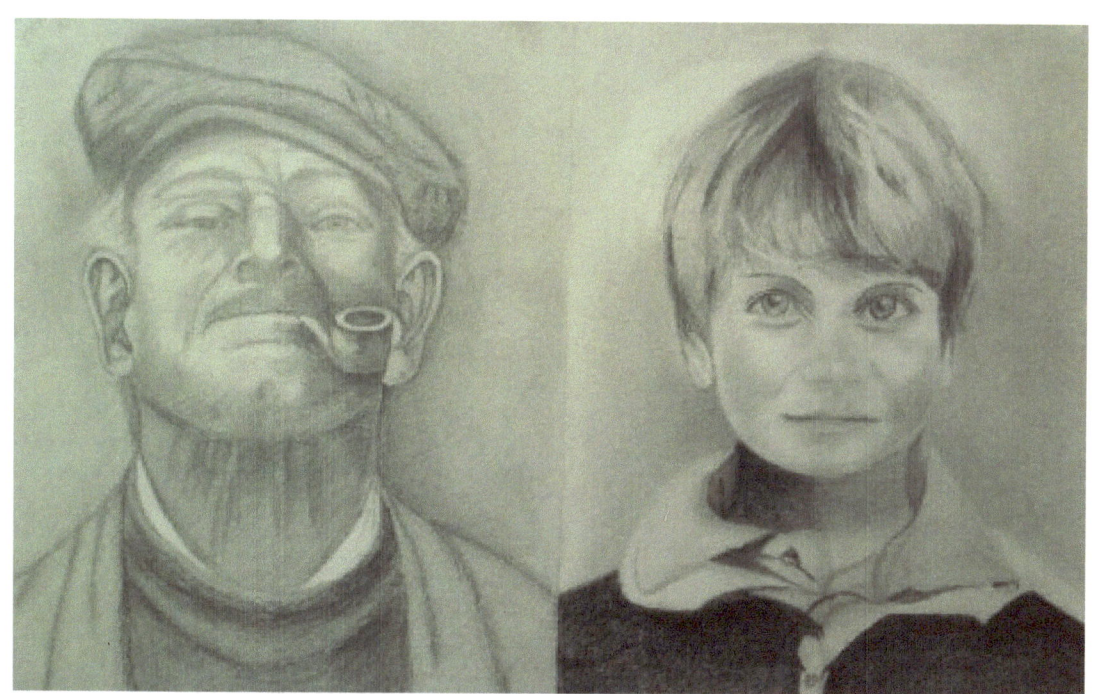

A little boy and a sailor man.

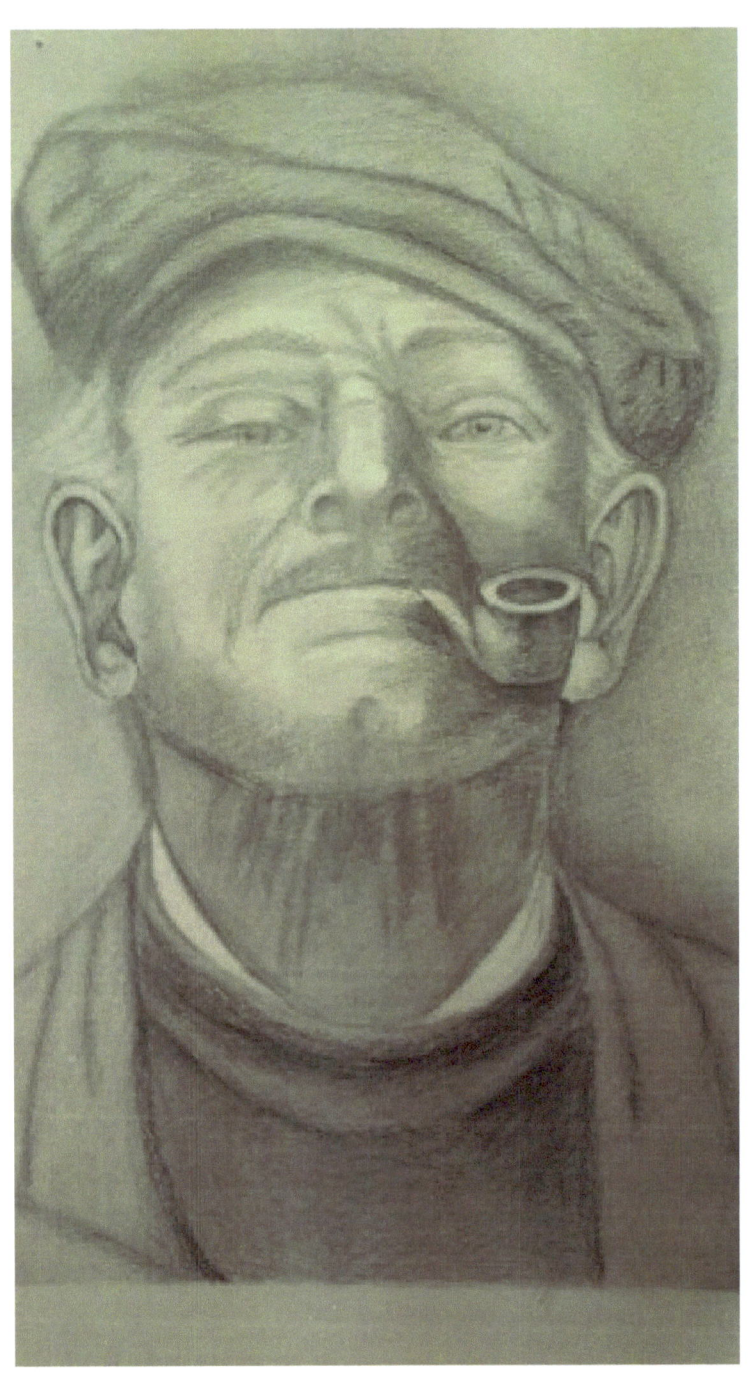

A sailor man.

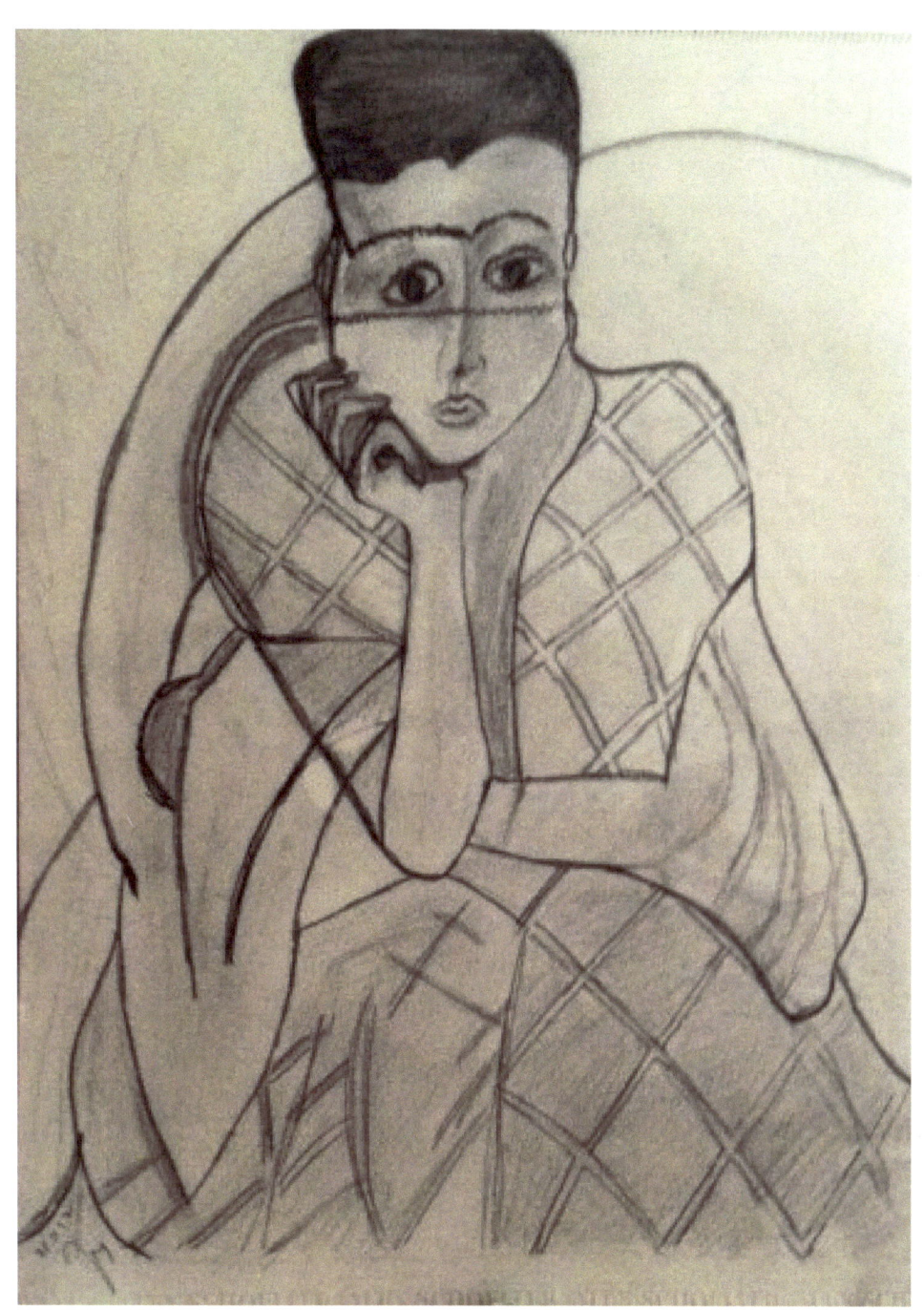

The mask.

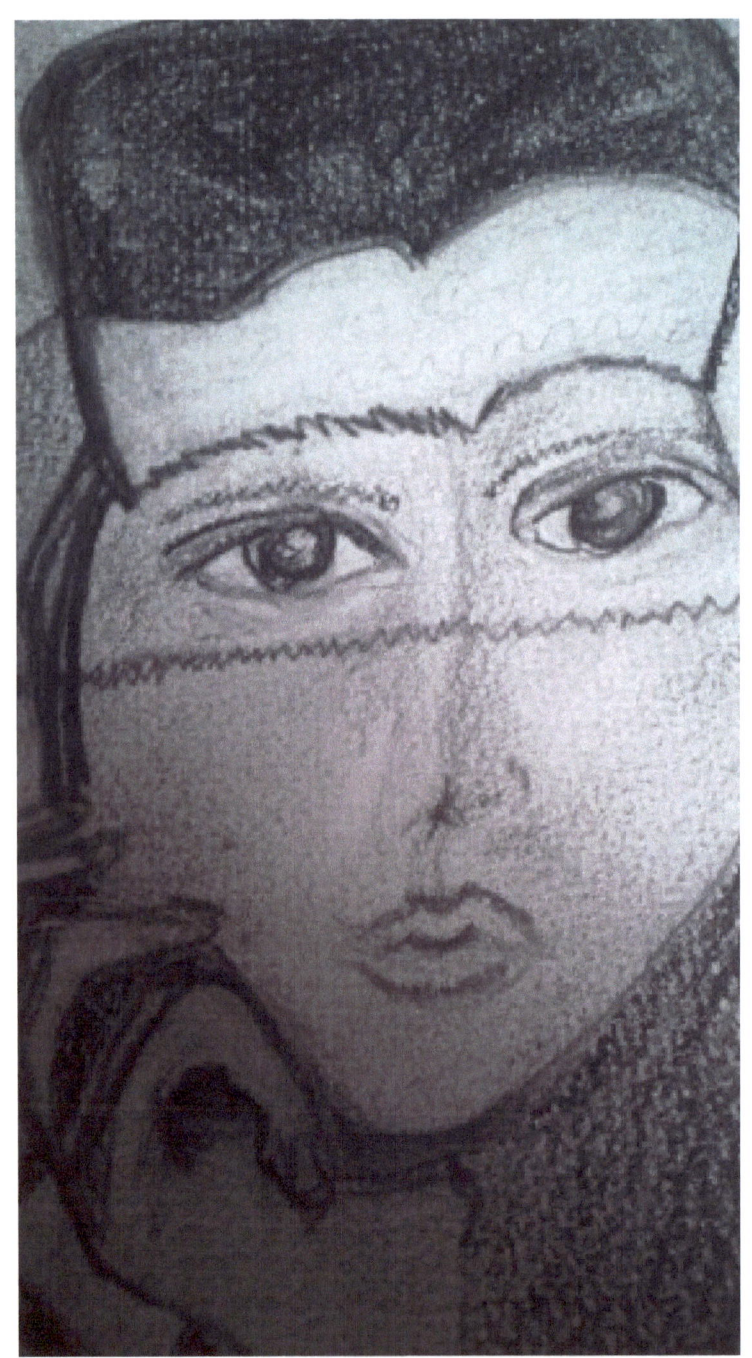

The mask .Detail

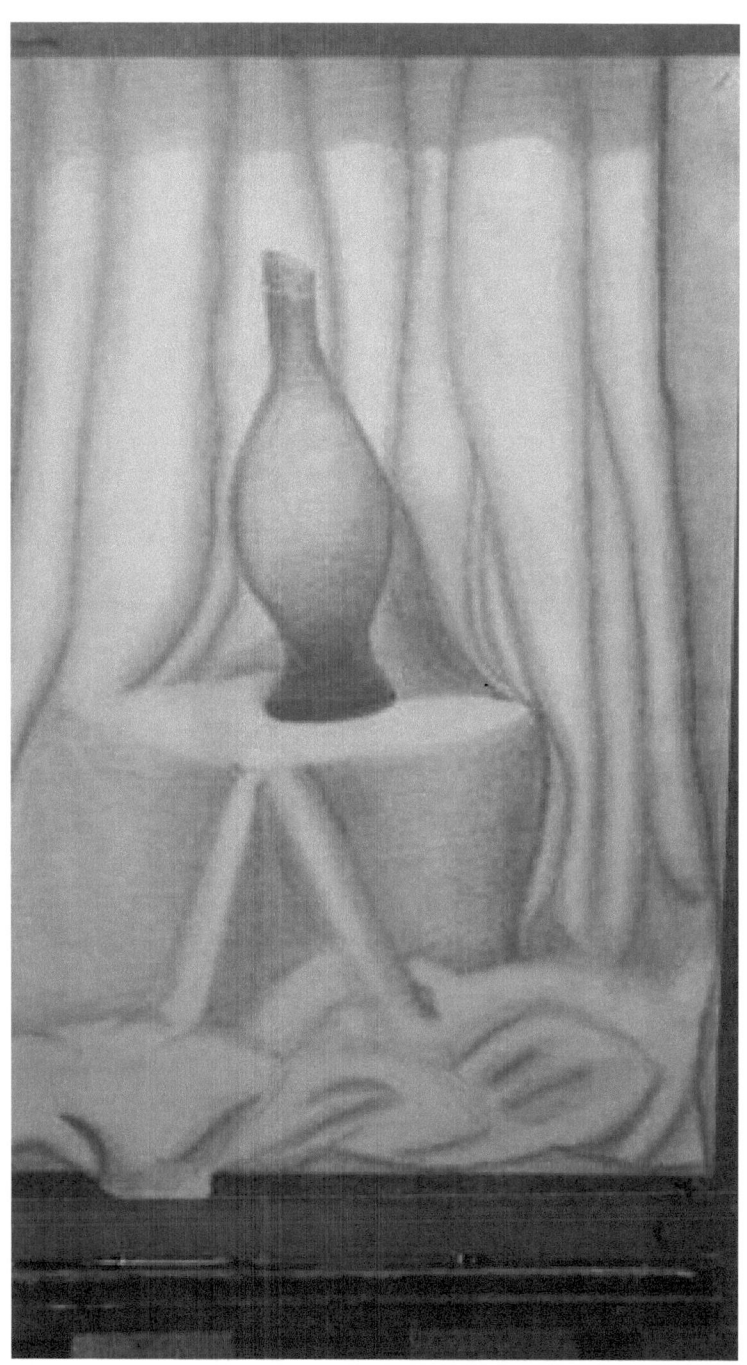

A bottle

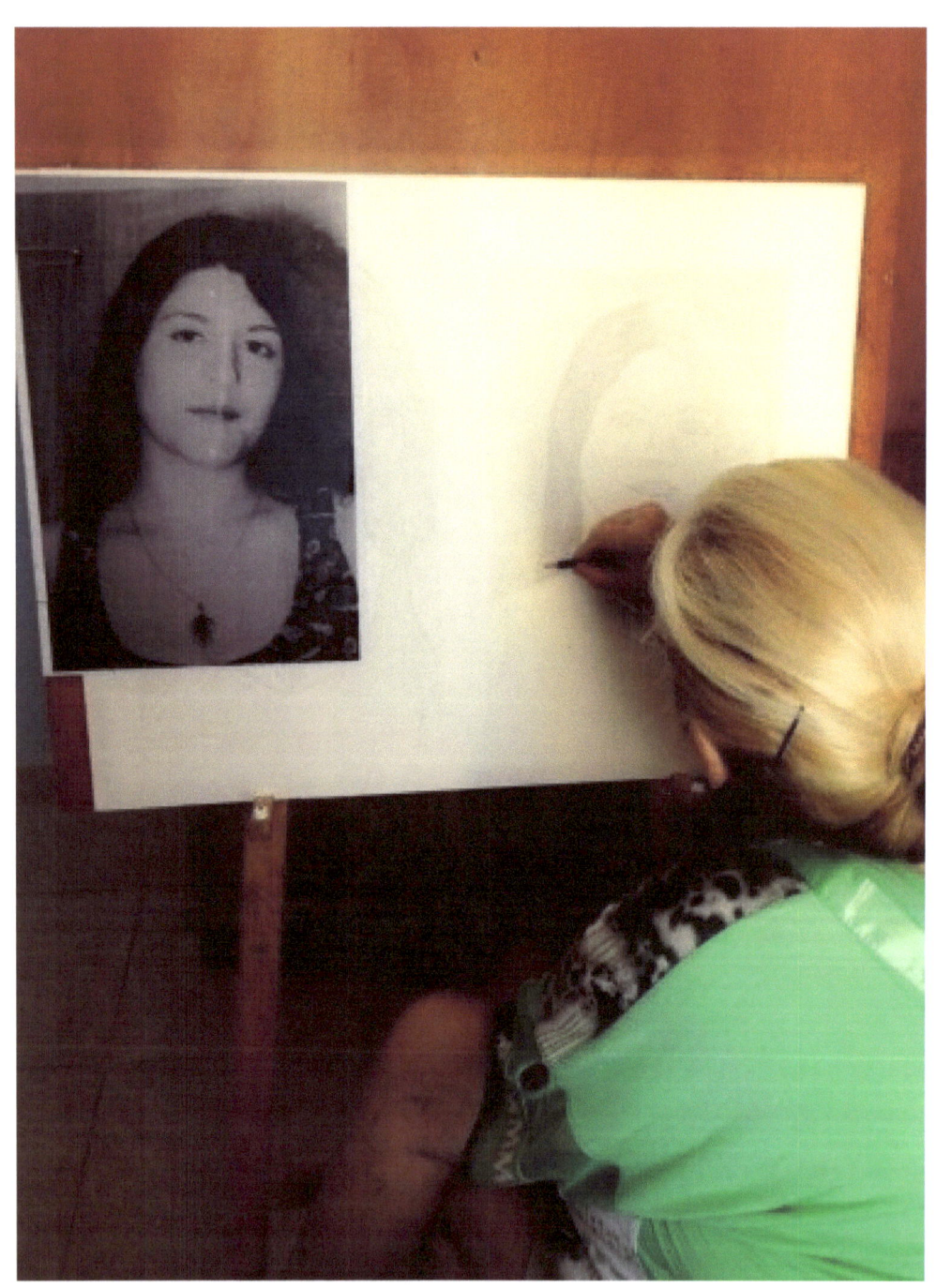

Drawing in progress

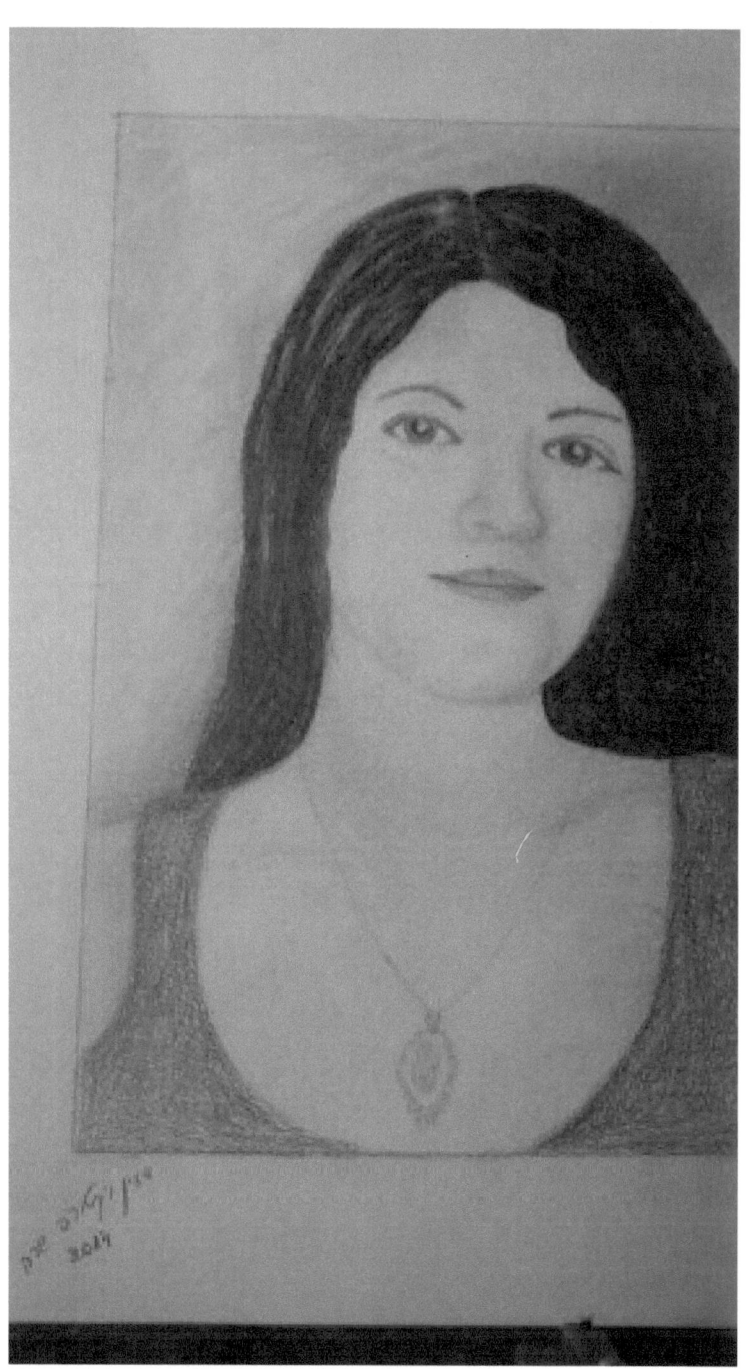

My self portrait

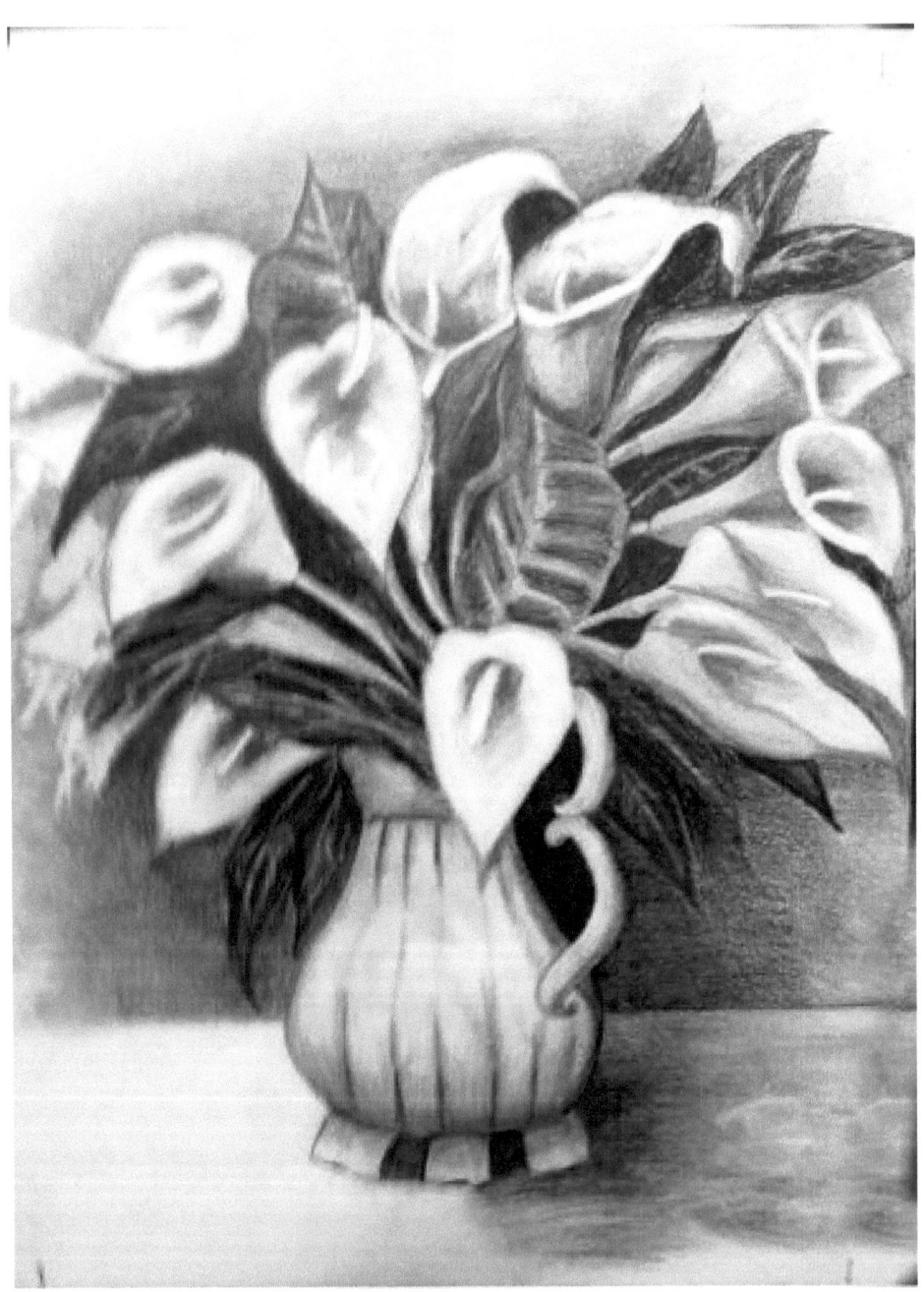

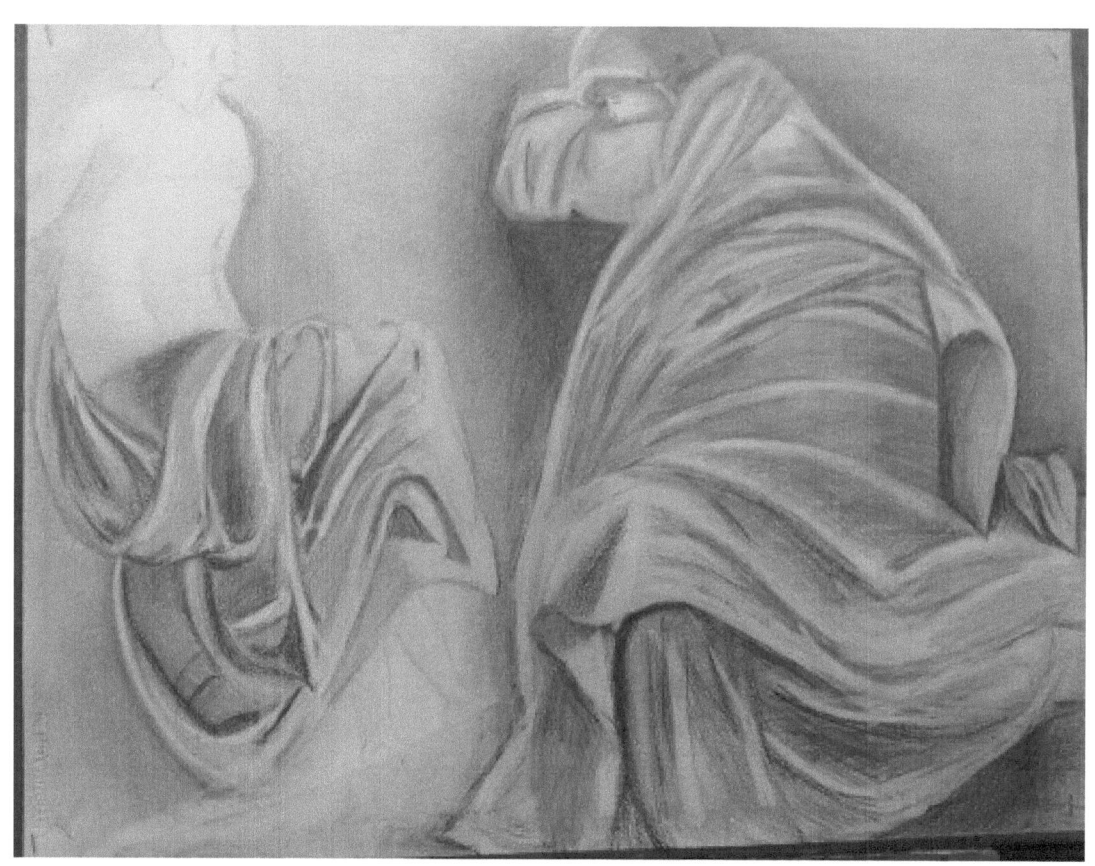

My pencil drawing inspired by Michelangelo Buonarroti.

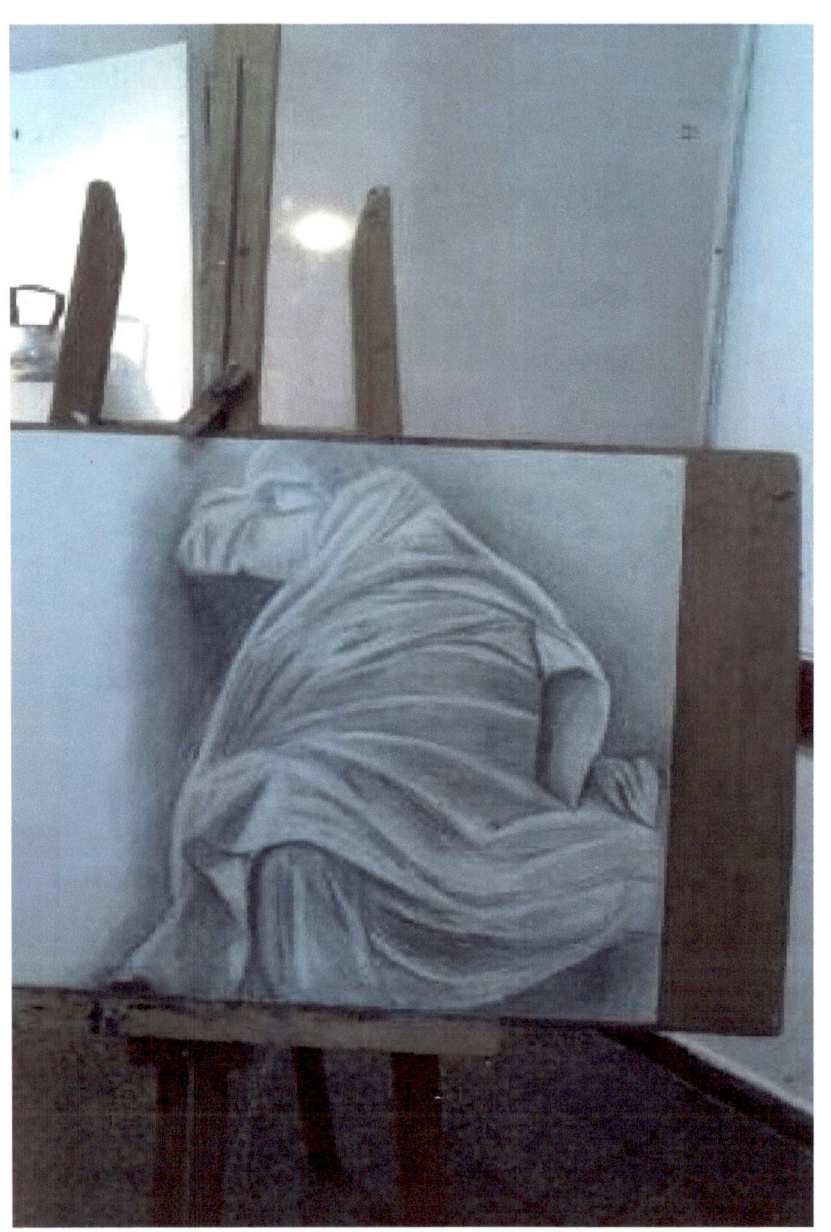

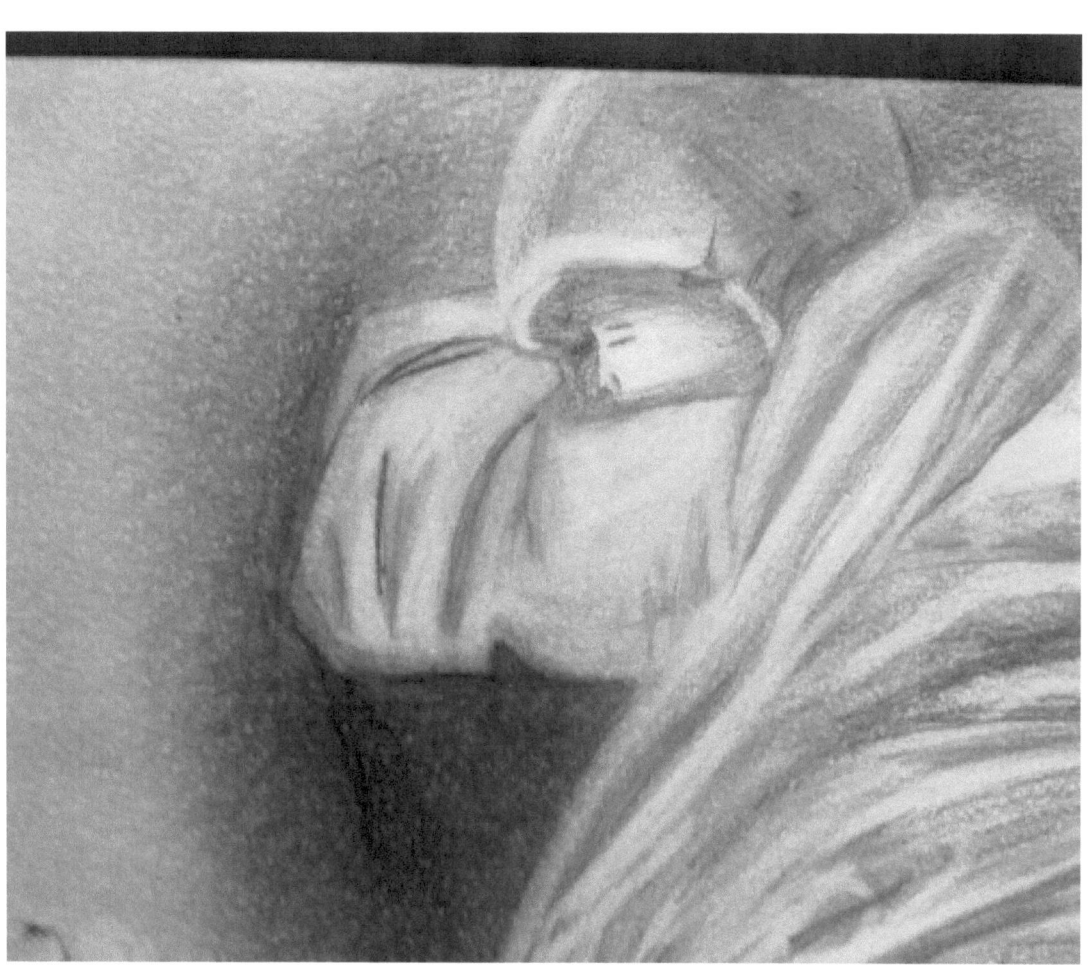

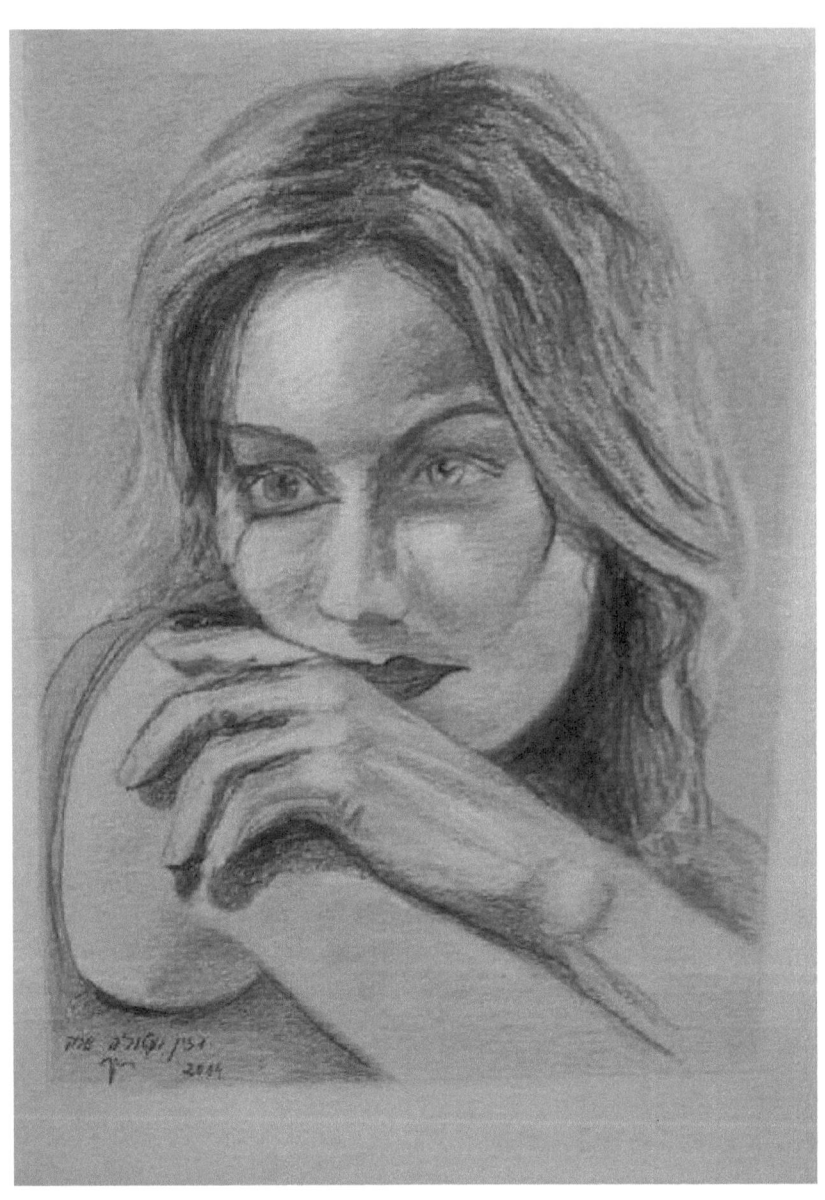

A young woman

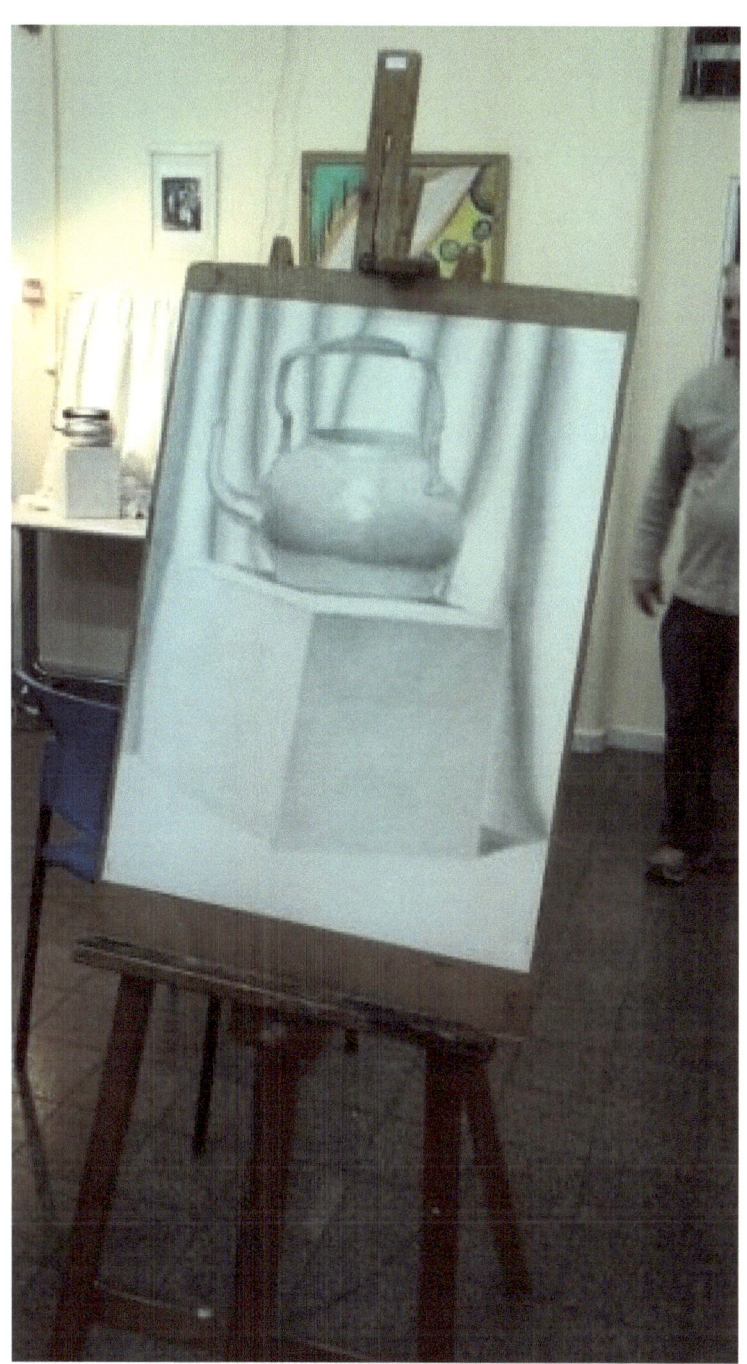

Drawing in progress

Part 2
Drawings in color pencils

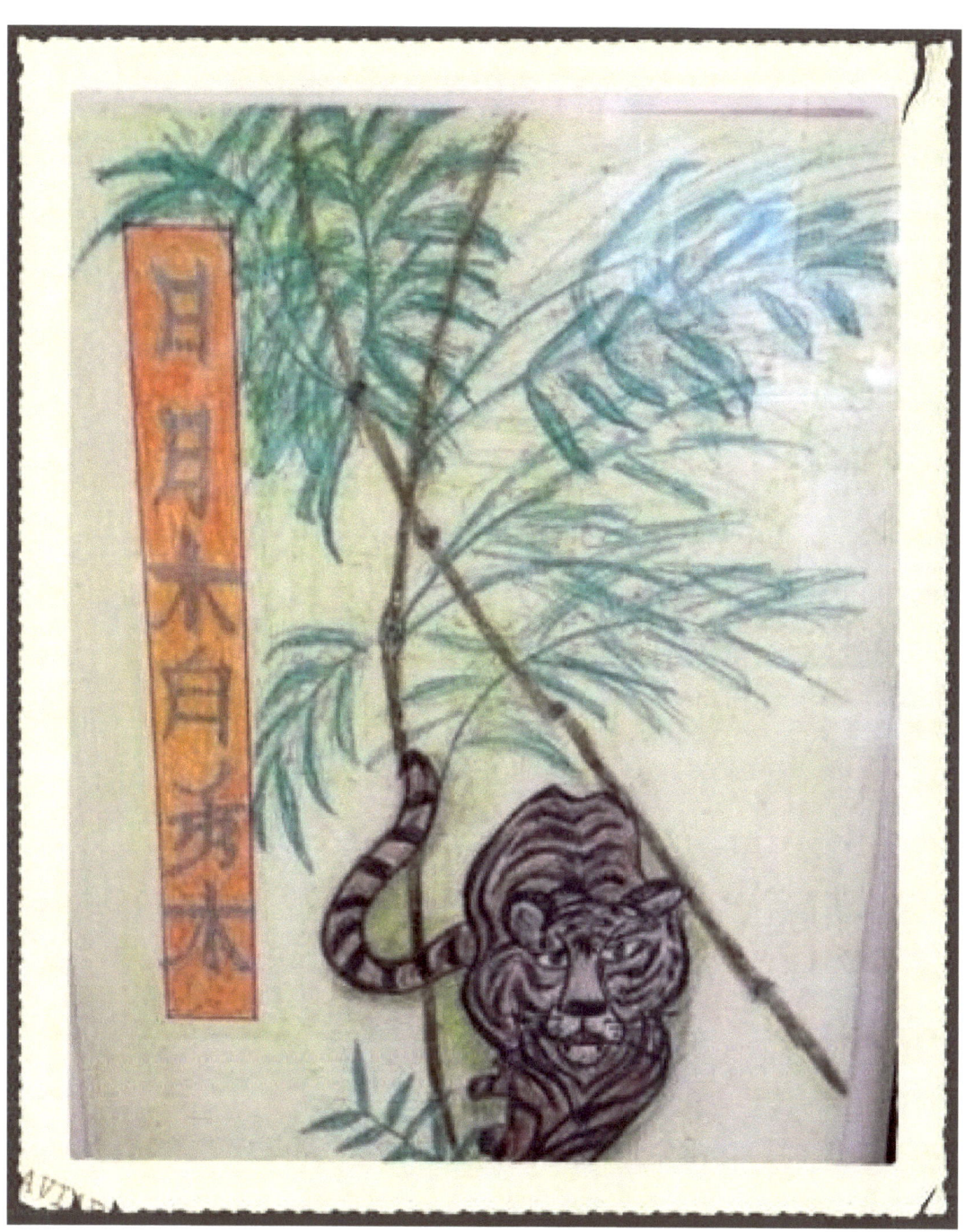

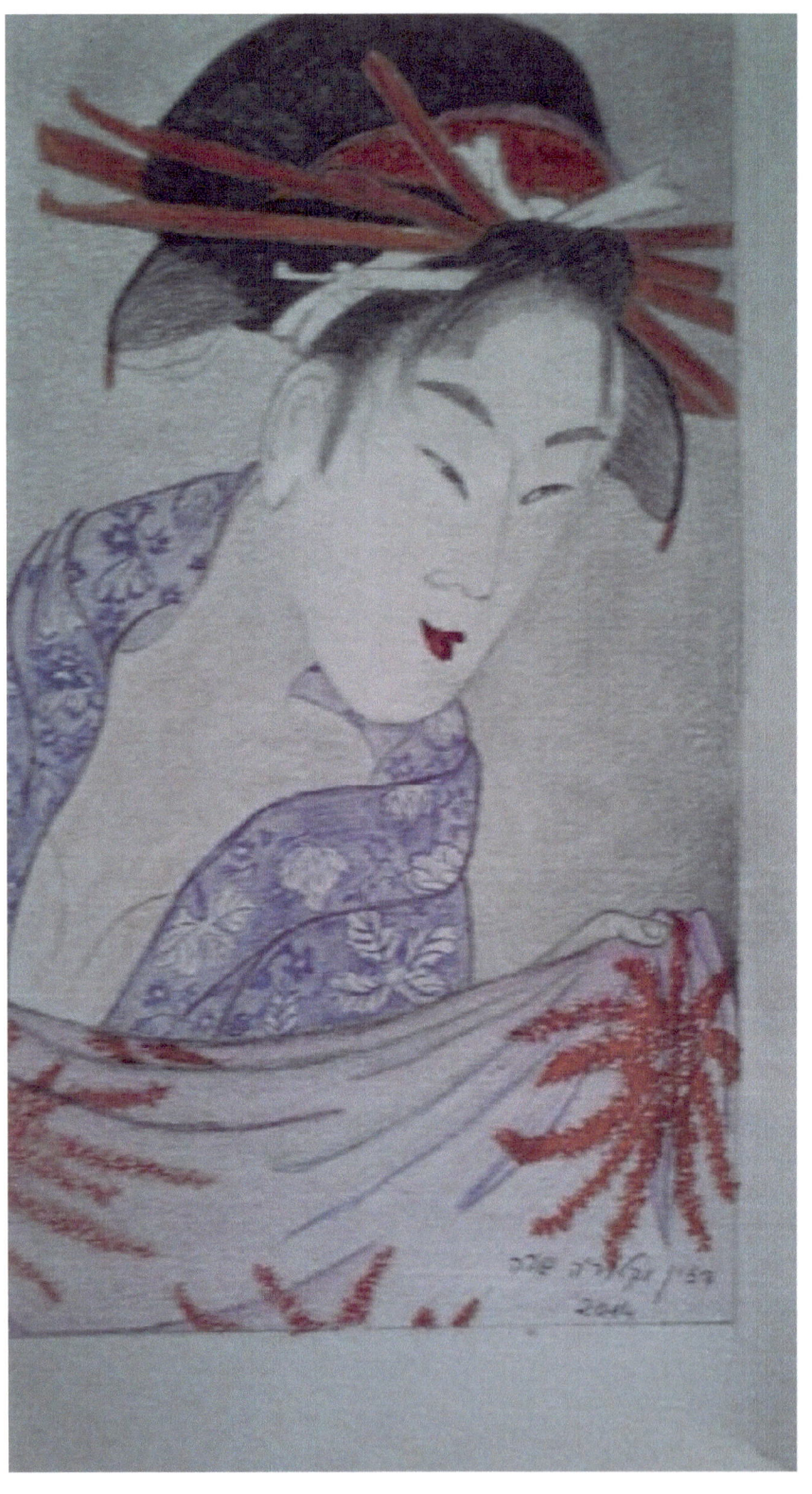

Part 3

Pastel oil on paper

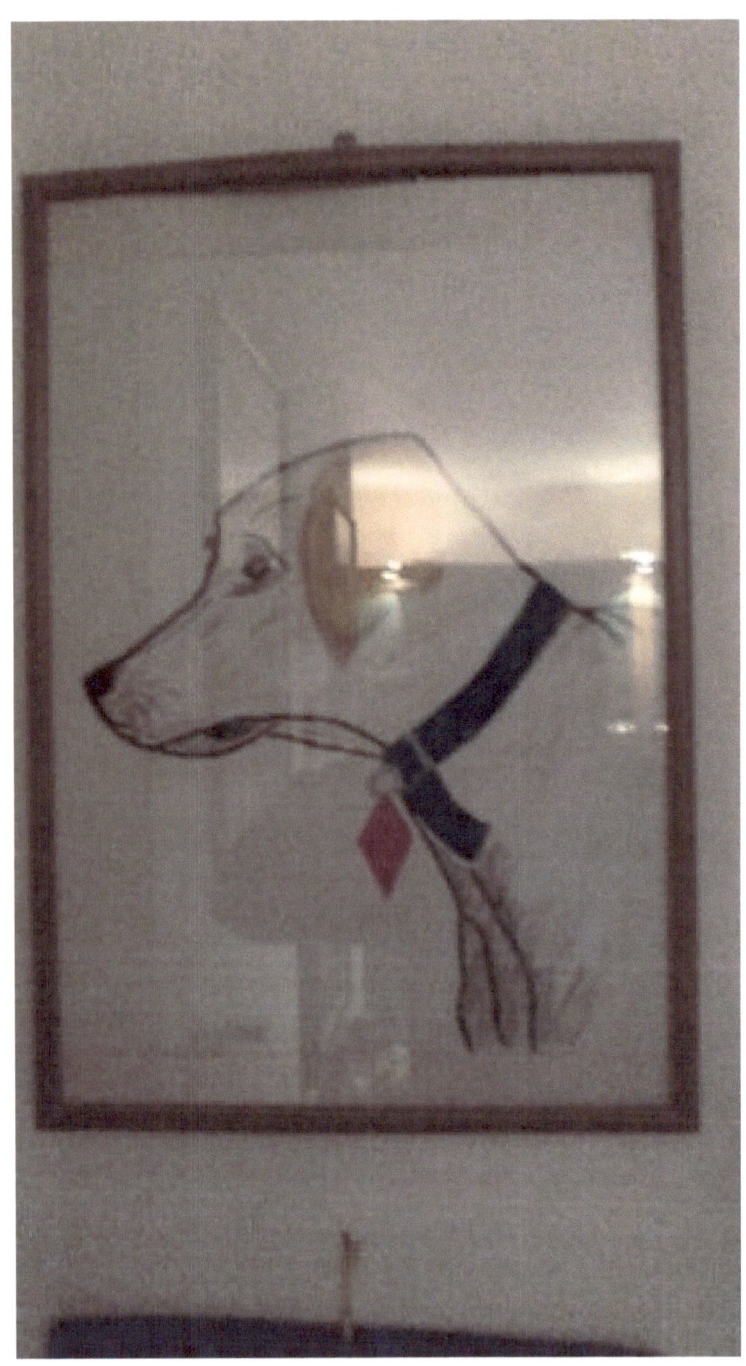

My dog Mika. She was 6 months old at the time. (2003).

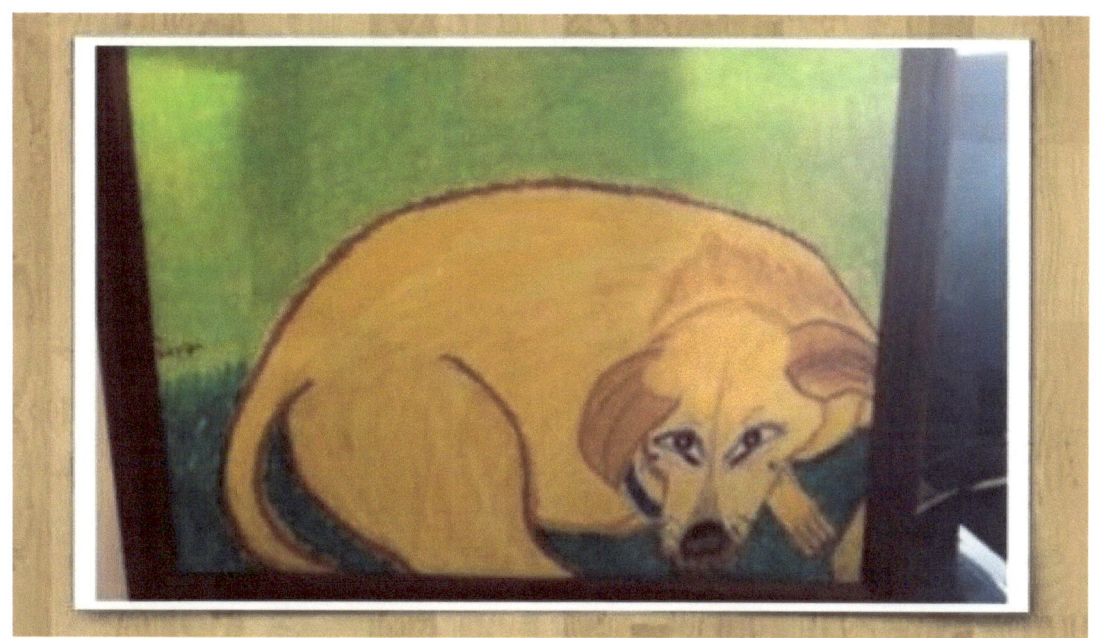

Mika in 2007. She died in 2012 after a long illness

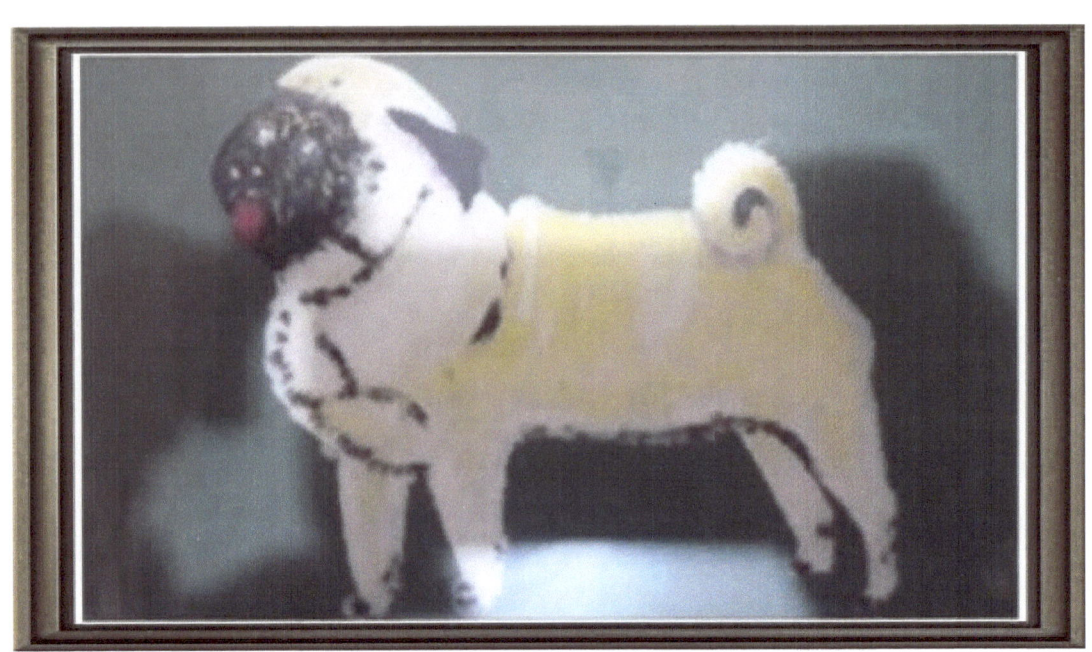

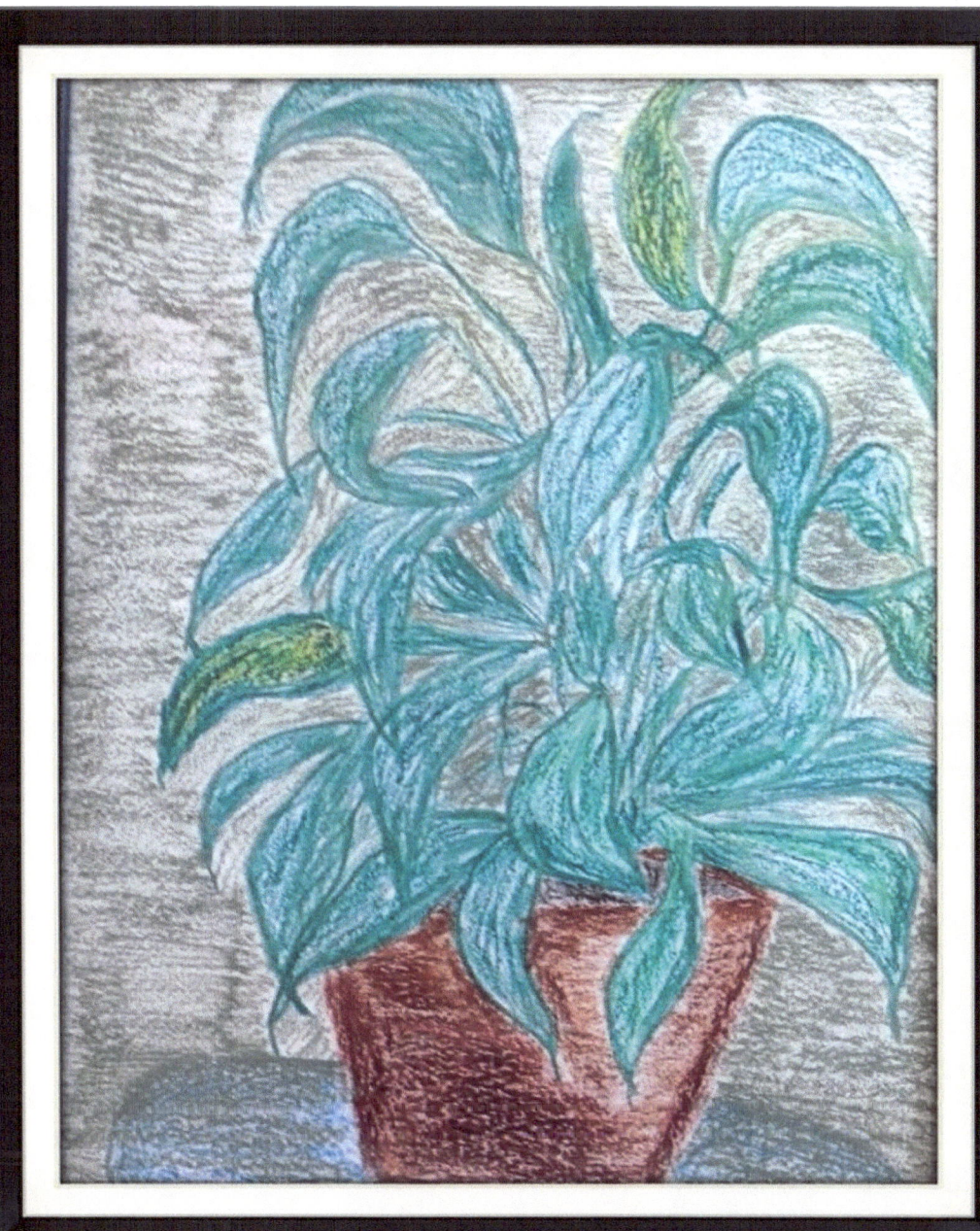

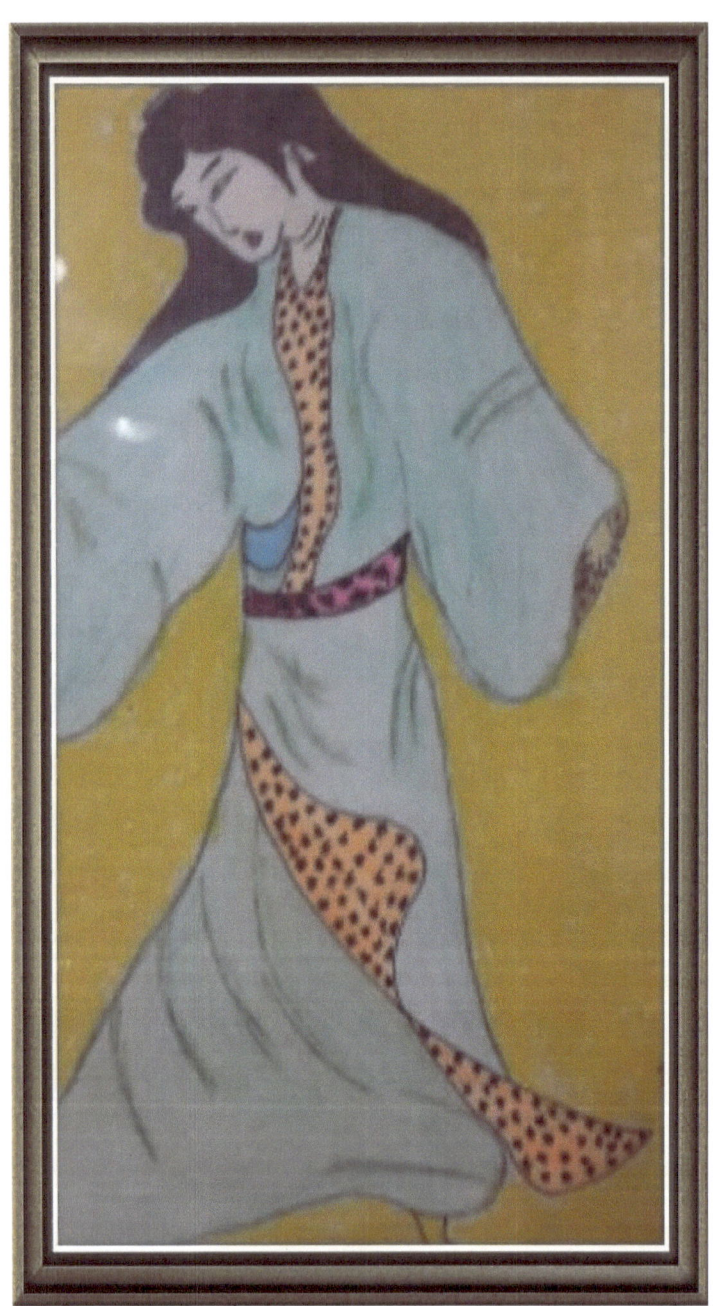

Japanese woman

Part 4

Aquarelle paintings

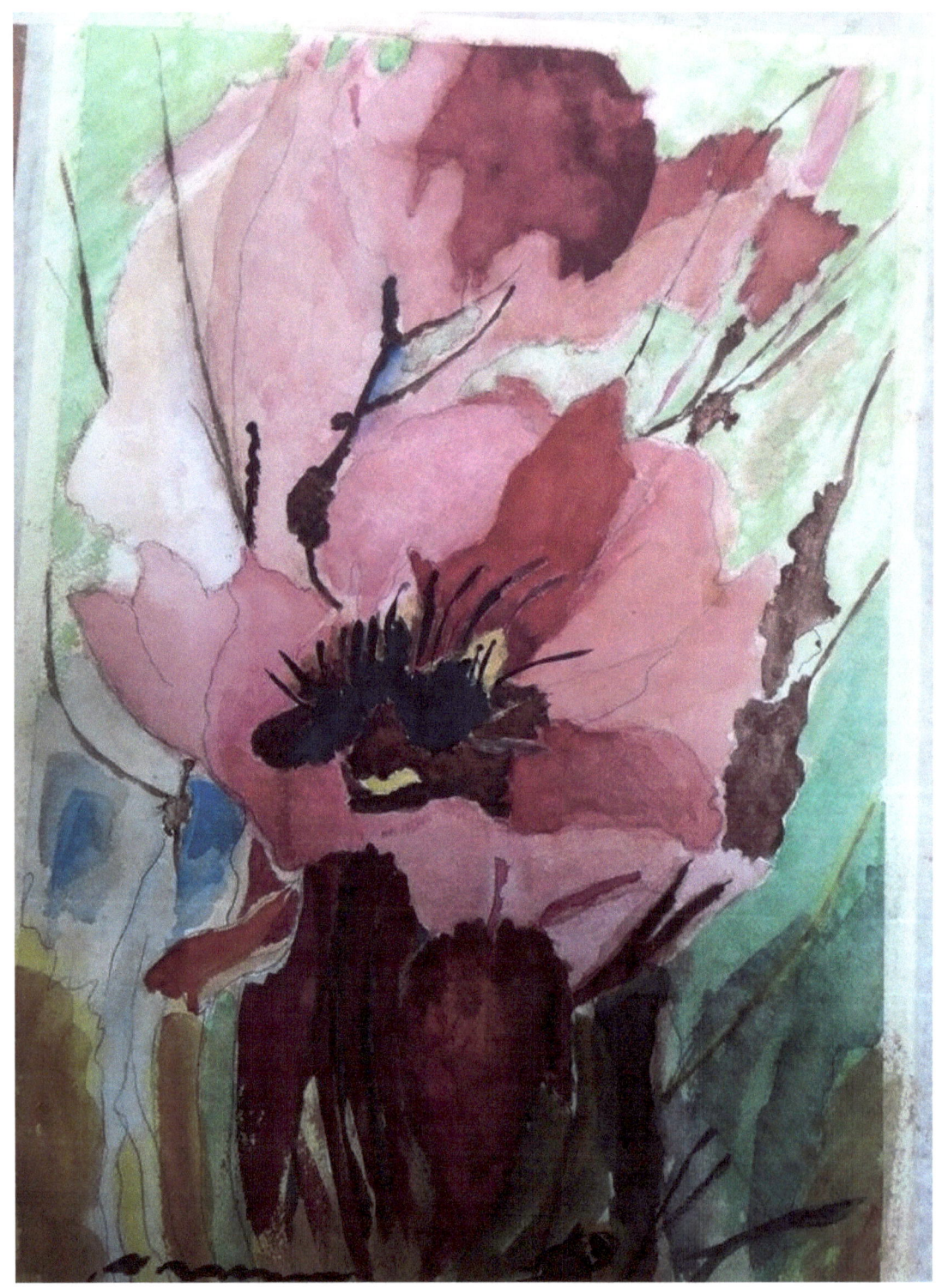

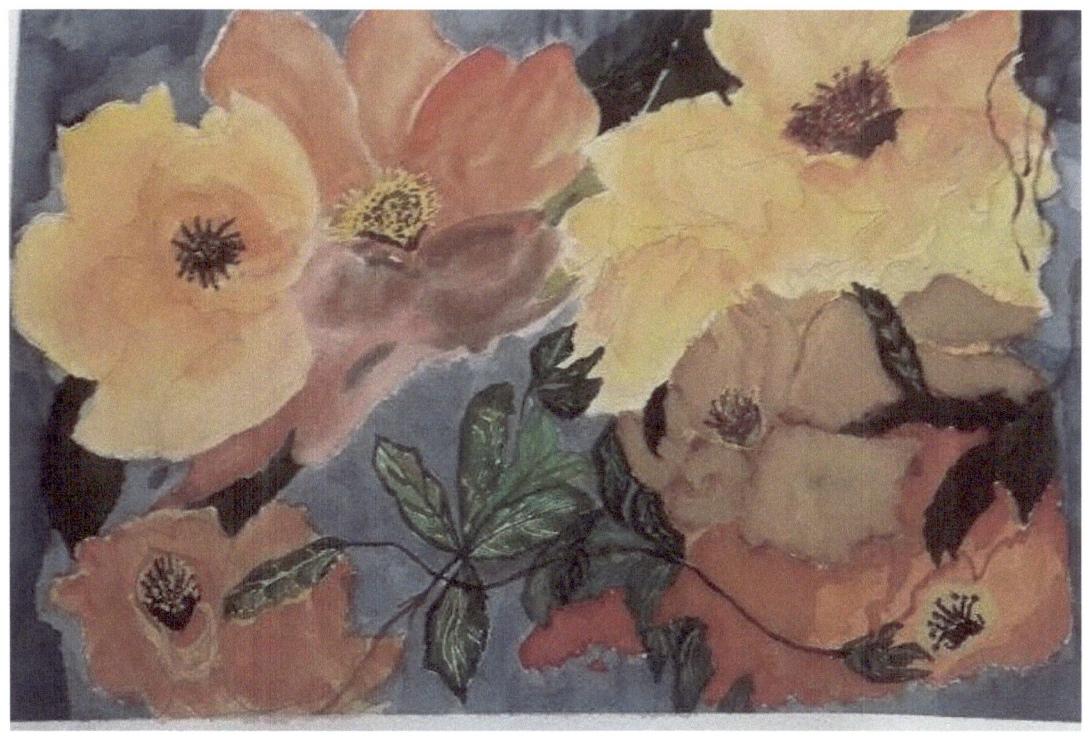

Roses

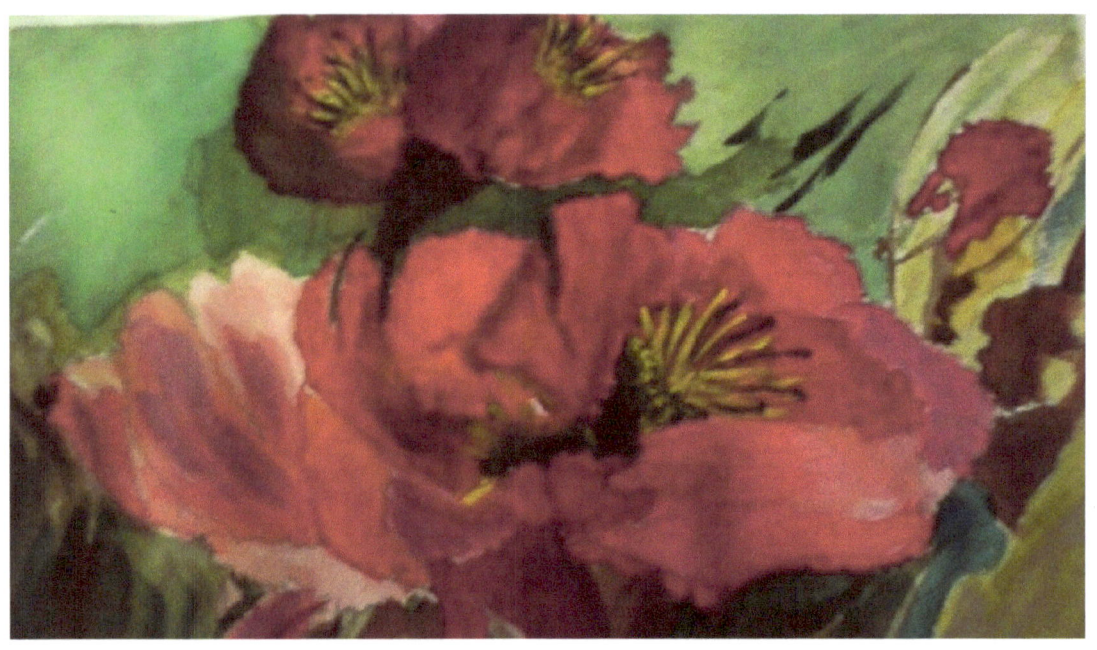

Roses

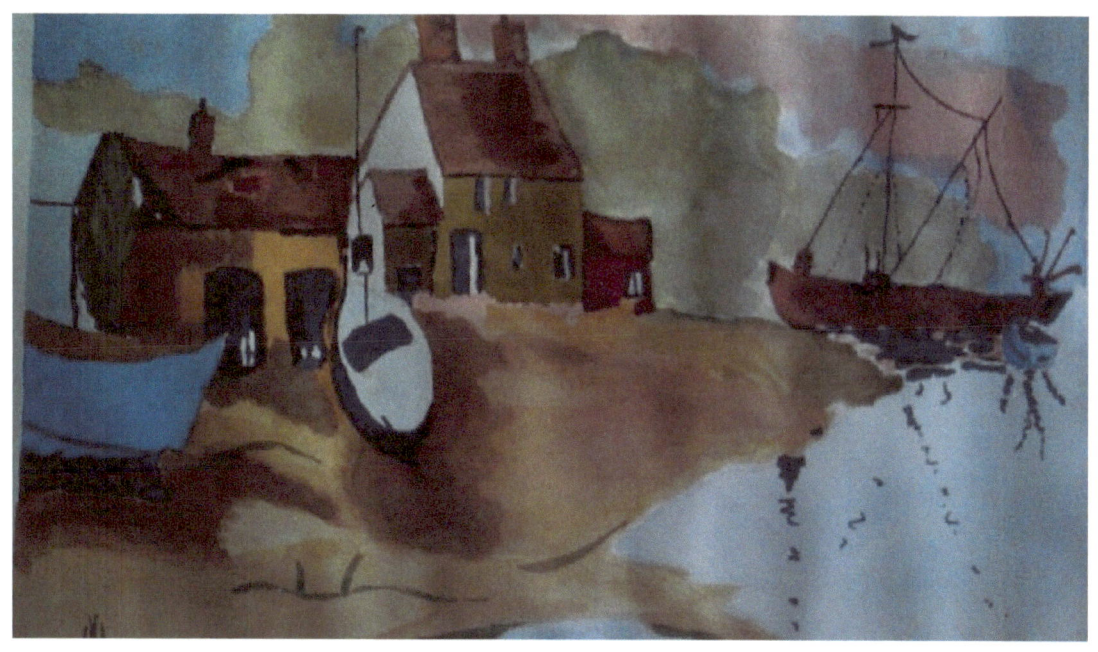

Cape Cod

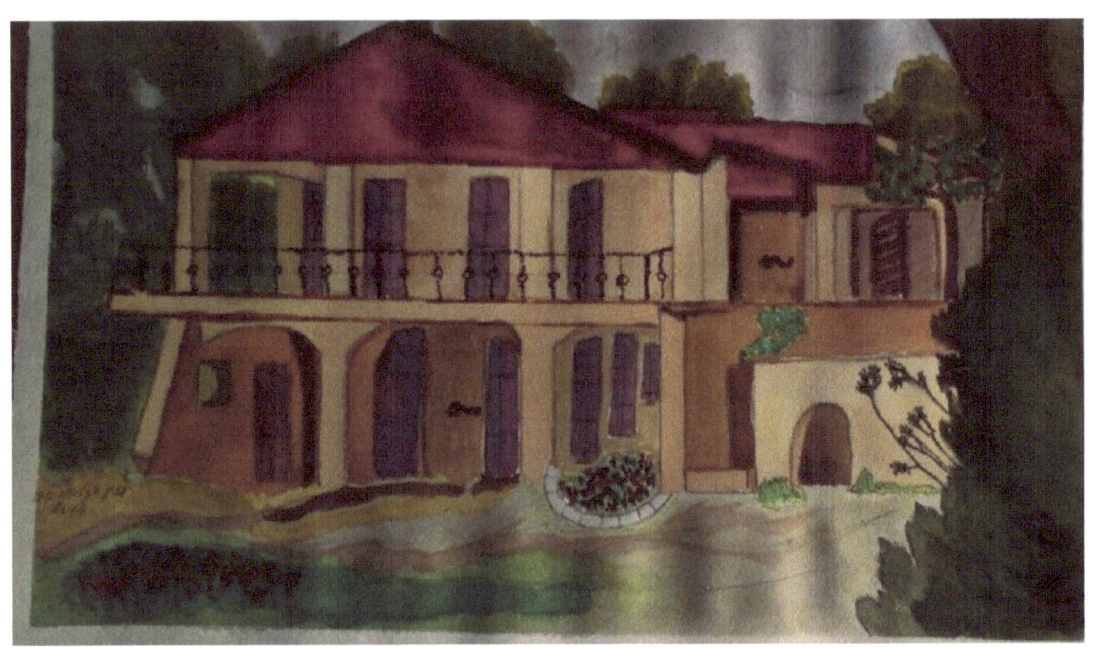

Home sweet home

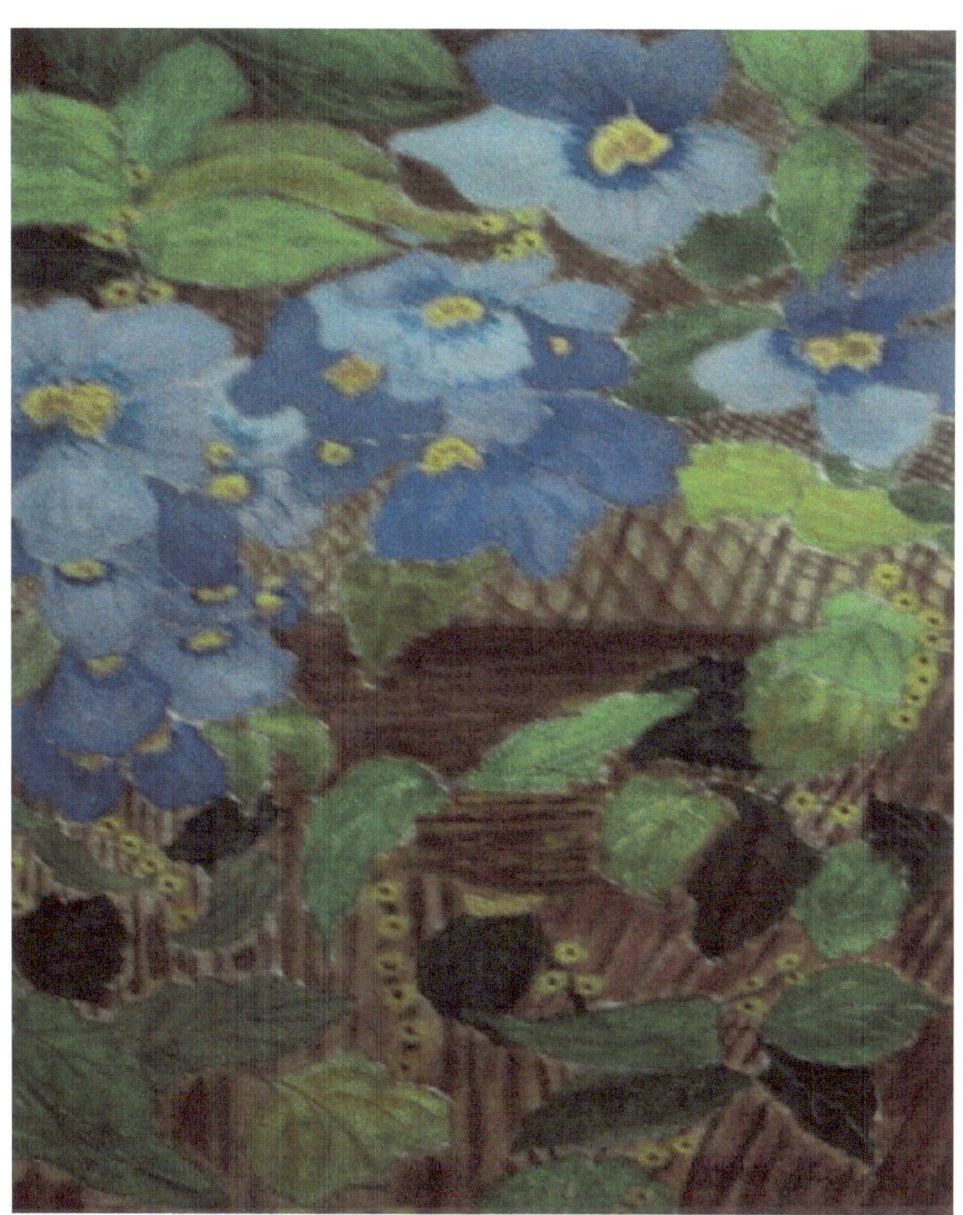

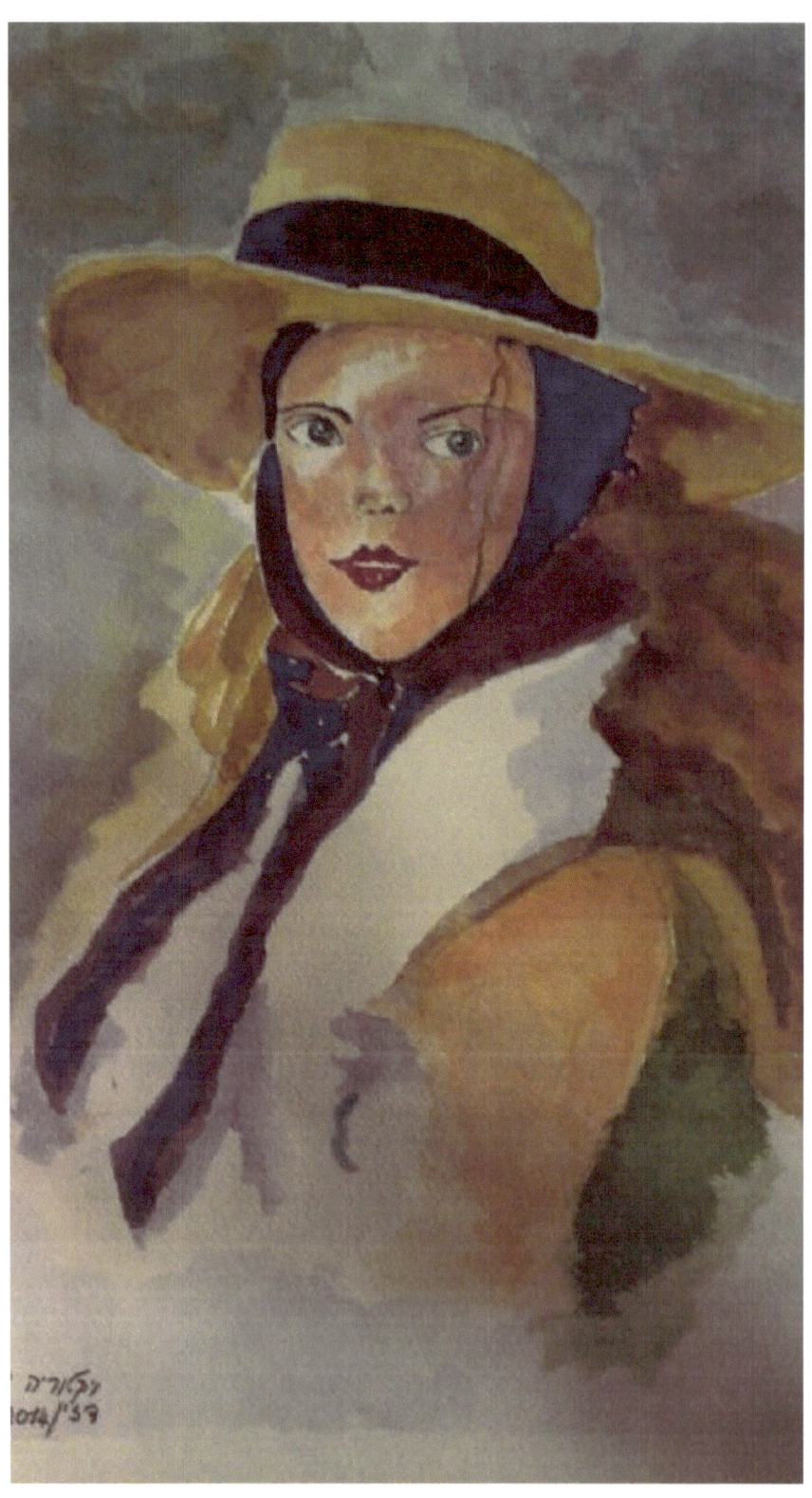

עליזה יורק
2014/'59

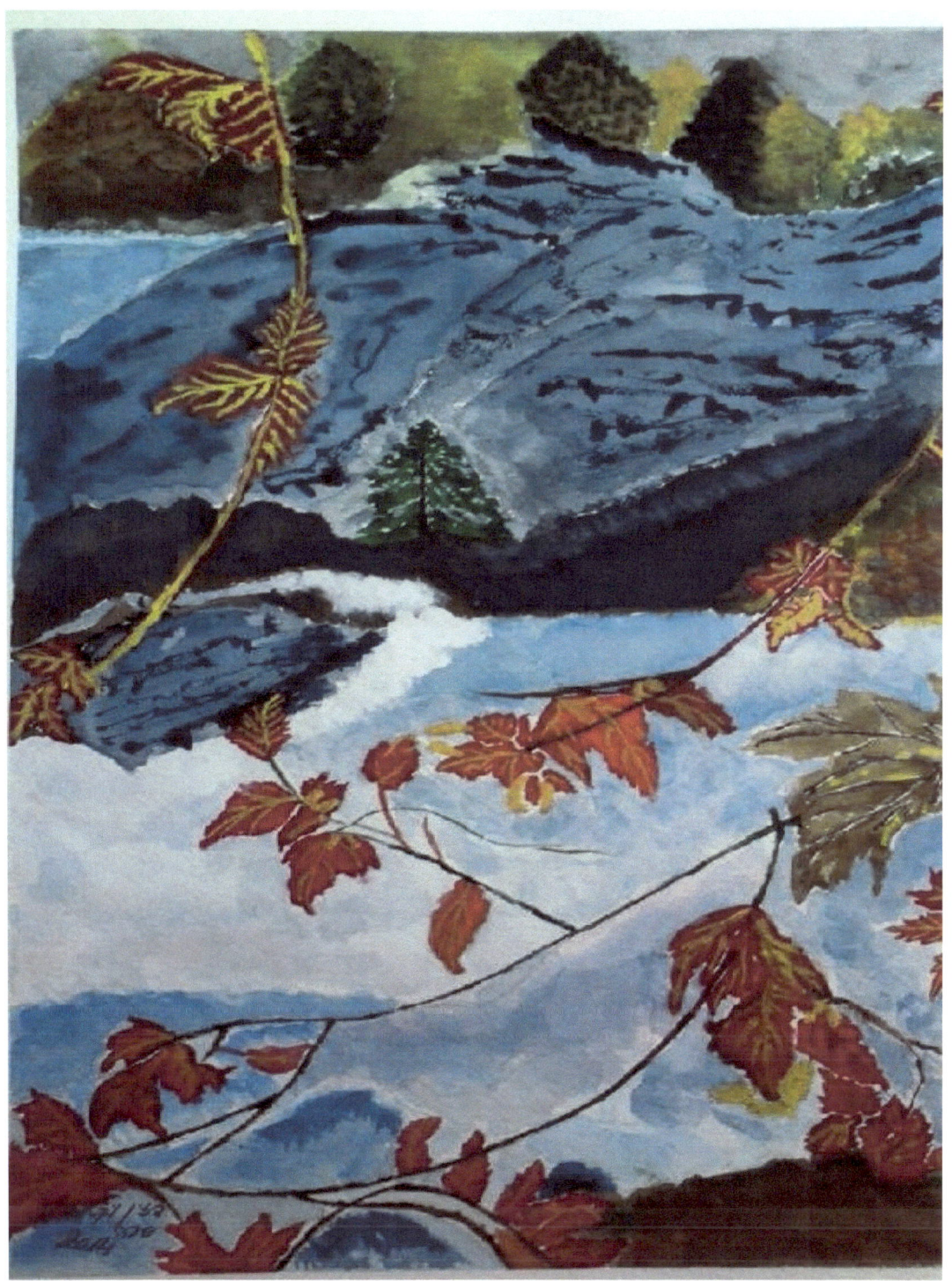

Part 5
Oil colors paintings

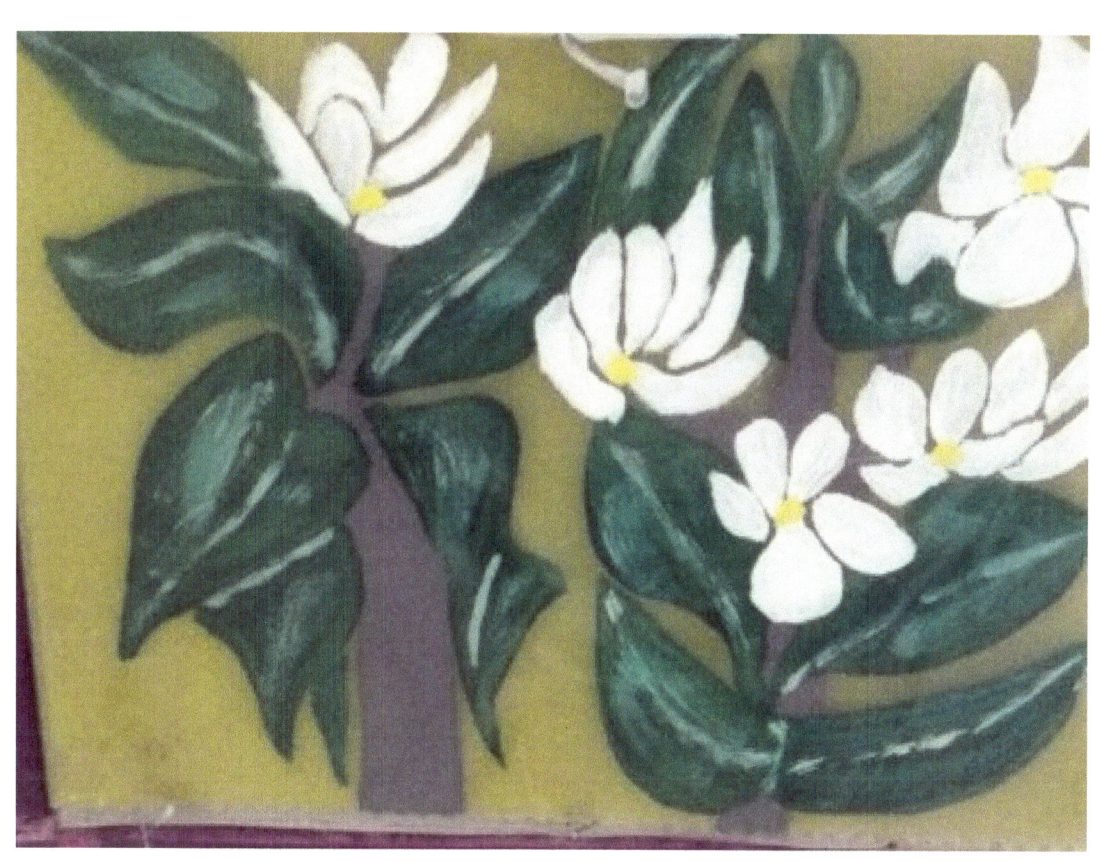

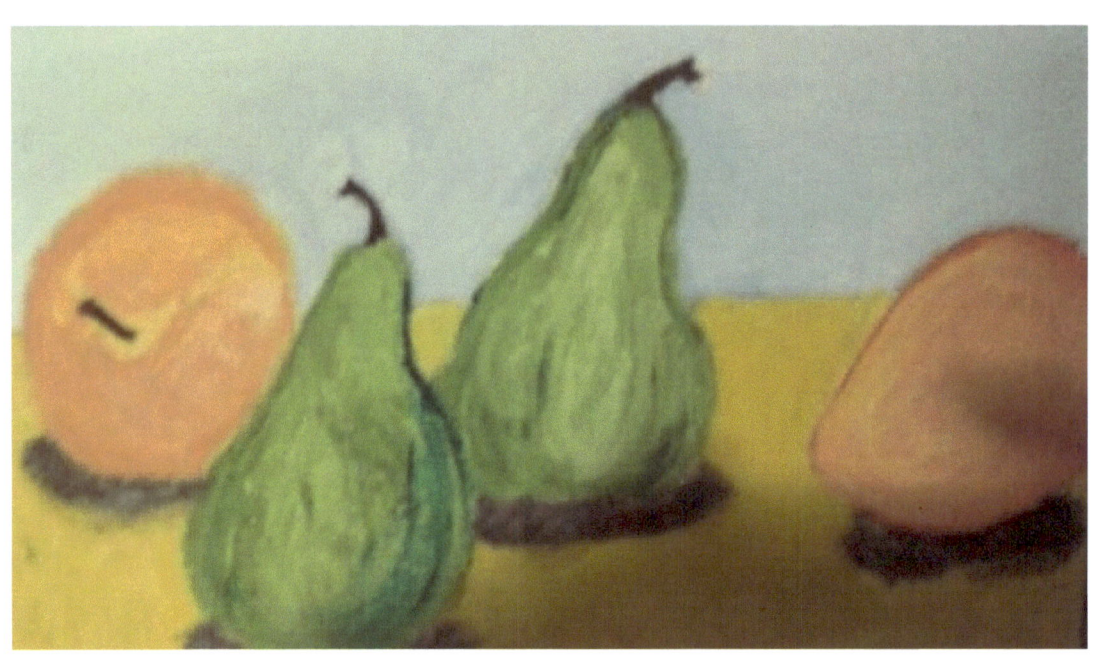

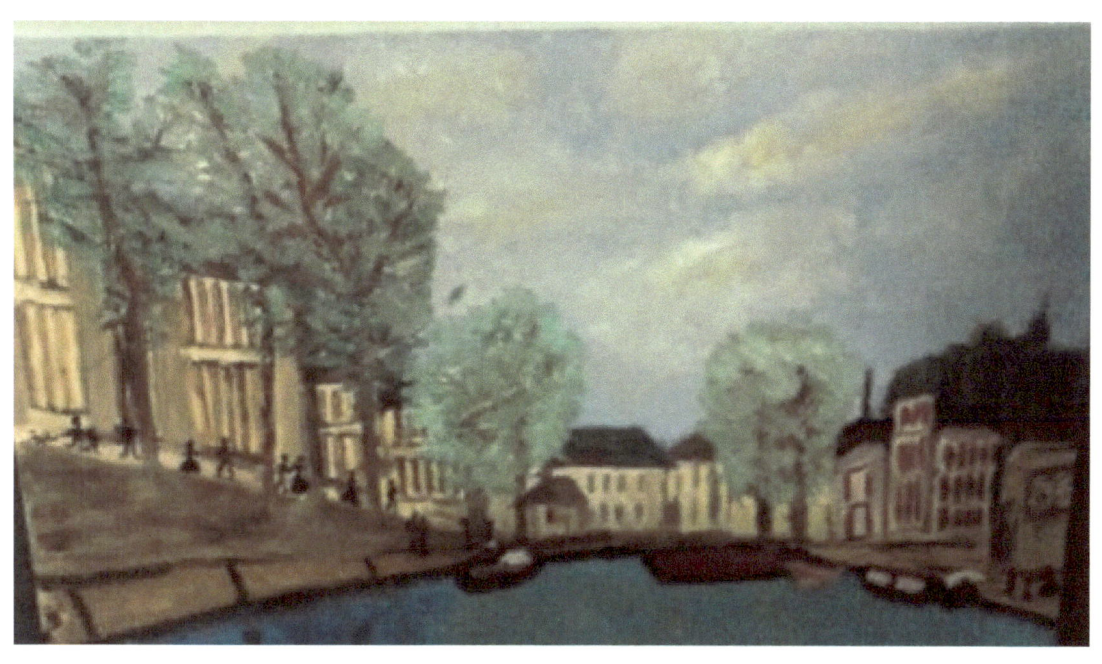

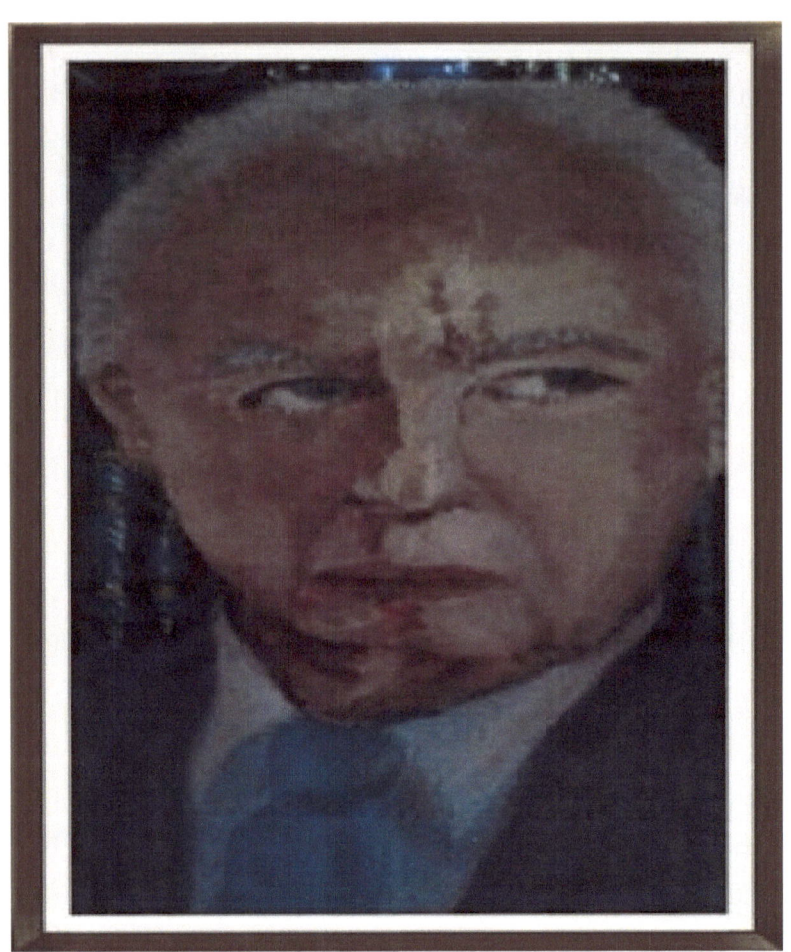

Yitzhak Rabin (1922- 1995).

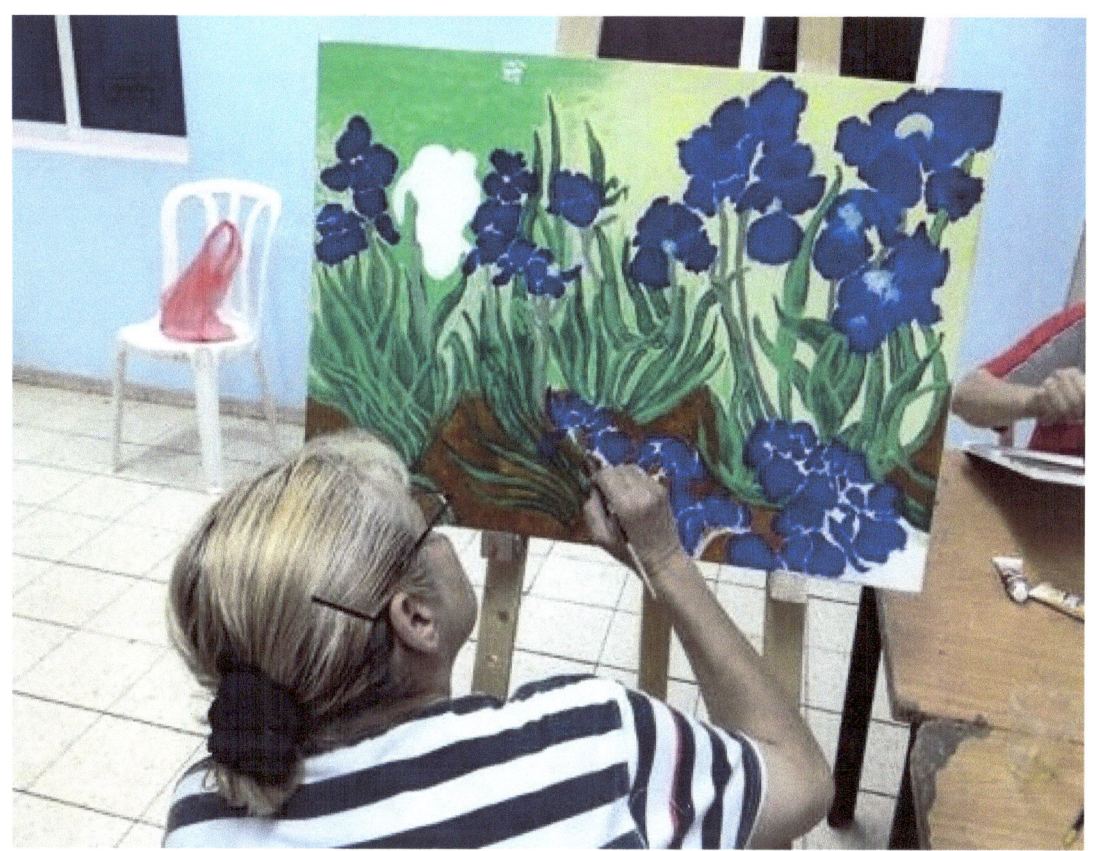

Painting in progress

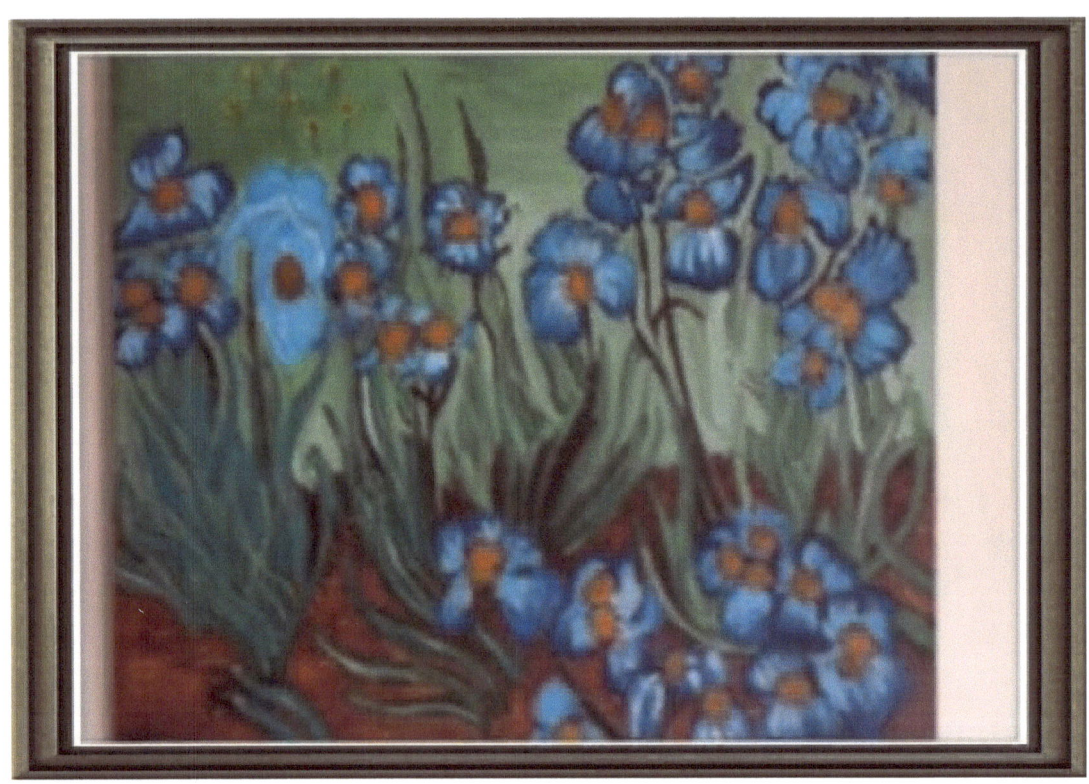

Inspirited by Van Gogh